# SOCIAL PHILOSOPHY

# Social Philosophy

THOMAS McPHERSON
*Reader in Philosophy,*
*University College, Cardiff*

VAN NOSTRAND REINHOLD COMPANY
LONDON
NEW YORK   CINCINNATI   TORONTO   MELBOURNE

VAN NOSTRAND REINHOLD COMPANY LTD
Windsor House, 46 Victoria Street, London, S.W.1.

INTERNATIONAL OFFICES
New York  Cincinnati  Toronto  Melbourne

Library of Congress Catalog Card No. 72-125953
SBN 442 05296 0
*First published 1970*

Printed in Great Britain by
The Archway Press, Bournemouth.

## PREFACE

THIS book is an introduction to a subject which is increasingly being studied at the present time — for instance, by those preparing for a Diploma in Social Science. However, it is not meant to be a textbook. There is no pretence to an exhaustive treatment of the subject matter. The book will, I hope, be seen as calling attention to some important questions rather than as providing conveniently neat answers to them; many, indeed, are questions that simply do not allow neat answers. The aim is that the book should be of use to readers who want some idea of the nature of the questions about man in society that philosophers discuss and of the typical ways in which they discuss them. Those who want to go on from here will find help in the Bibliography.

Chapter 7 incorporates an article ('Punishment: Definition and Justification') published in *Analysis* **28**, 21—27 (1967); I am grateful to the editor of *Analysis* for agreeing to its reappearance here. I wish to thank my colleague Vernon Pratt for reading the typescript: he made many valuable comments, from which I have profited, though he is not to be held responsible for the faults that remain. I should like also to thank Sheila Spencer, Sue Vaughan, and Bridget Moloney, who typed the manuscript.

*Cardiff,*
*May 1970.*                                                          T.McP.

# CONTENTS

CHAPTER 1

# Social Philosophy and Social Science

SOCIAL science is new. In the Western tradition, speculation about society goes back as far as the Ancient Greeks; but although the contribution of the Greeks to the understanding of man in society was considerable, we do not say that they were social scientists. It might be suggested that they were not social scientists simply because they were not scientists; and this certainly contains some element of truth. Our very notion of what constitutes science derives in large part from the advance in the natural sciences in the seventeenth century: let a thing be done with great success and that success tends to set the standard for what it means to be that thing. 'Science' means the work of Galileo and of Newton. Whatever went before tends to be seen as at best primitive science, at worst not science at all. However unhistorical this popular picture may be, however disparaging of the work of these men's predecessors (including the Greeks), it still has much force. Where we do not expect to see science we do not see it. Only when science had taken a spectacular step forward in the seventeenth century could men begin to be clear about scientific method. Not until then therefore could they even raise the question whether there could be a social science. This is certainly one reason why we may say that there was no social science in Ancient Greece — the same reason that has led people to say, though mistakenly, that there was no science *simpliciter* in Ancient Greece.

However, although this may satisfy some people well enough as far as the Greeks are concerned, we can hardly find an excuse in these terms for the seventeenth century itself. When science made its 'real' beginning, it was still not in the form of social science. 'The proper study of mankind is man.' No doubt. But the *scientific* study of man

1

took a long time to come into existence, and the scientific study of social man has only begun to develop fully in our own century. Why is this so? Why was not the great leap forward in the natural sciences accompanied by a beginning of the social sciences? To some extent, of course, a few first steps were taken, but a few steps do not constitute an advance.

The growth of social science was hampered at the outset by the obstacle of individualism. The stumbling block was the failure to take society seriously. The Greeks may have lacked something on the side of science, but at least they recognised the importance of the social nature of man. It is this recognition that is missing in a writer like Hobbes. The individualism of the seventeenth century was to continue long. It did not hinder the development of some studies that have since become social sciences — economics and psychology — but at that time and for long subsequently these were sciences with an individualistic bias. The scientific study of society had to wait upon the recognition of the importance of society. As long as the basic unit is taken to be the individual, and instead of society what is seen is only collections of individuals, social science can make no fruitful advance. What is a little surprising about the individualistic stress of Hobbes and, a little later, Locke, is that on one level it ran counter to the emphasis of their own society; for the natural human unit in Stuart England was not the individual but the family (see Laslett (2), p.19).

The shift in the focus of interest from society to the individual is one of the most striking differences between the Greeks and the seventeenth century writers. Of the reasons for this shift some, no doubt, were religious (the effect of Protestant Christianity, with its emphasis on the importance of the individual soul), some economic (competitive market relations: cf. Macpherson). We may be sure that whatever they were the reasons were mixed, and that there is no simple answer to the question of how the change came about. Fortunately, for our purposes we need not inquire how it happened. It is enough that it did happen.

For Hobbes, whose *Leviathan* was published in 1651, men are by nature individuals. They may live in society but only by an effort can they be of society. Each man is fearful of his neighbours, whom he sees as sources of danger to his life. Men are by nature self-interested, and the natural state of man is one of war of every man against every man. Each desires to preserve his own life and to increase in possessions and honour. In the state of nature, however, the difficulties in the way of achieving these ends are insuperable. Men who are constantly looking over their shoulders for the assassin do not have a life worth living; they certainly have no opportunity to cultivate the arts of civilization. When Hobbes says that the state of nature — that is, the natural condition of man, or what man would be like it his life were not somehow forced into a different pattern — is a state of war of every man against every man, he does not, of course, mean that in the state of nature men would be engaged in actually fighting each other day and night. Wars are not like that. There are lulls in the fighting. You may be safe for the moment. The point is, however, that you can never be sure that you are safe. Man's 'natural' existence is a condition of total uncertainty and insecurity. Men are more or less equal, according to Hobbes; those who are lacking in brain may be well endowed with brawn, and vice versa. No one, therefore, can hope to come out permanently on top in the war of all against all. The only way to escape from this hopeless condition, Hobbes tells us, is for men to come together to form society and designate someone, or some body of men, as absolute Sovereign. They must submit utterly to the Sovereign, who will rule them through their fears and save them from themselves. They remain individuals, but accept a restriction on their freedom as individuals in order to achieve in the end what they find they cannot achieve without this restriction.

Locke also saw men as individuals, even if not with the whole-hearted consistency of Hobbes. Men are born with certain rights — to life, liberty, and possessions — and political society is a device that they set up in order to preserve those rights. The state of nature Locke saw not as a state of war but as one of freedom and mutual tolerance. Men are by nature moral beings, though it seems that the phrase 'by nature' here may not mean quite what it meant for Hobbes. The contrast between Hobbes and Locke is probably not a simple contrast between one man who thought that people are bad and another who thought that they are good. The contrast is between two senses of the phrase 'by nature'. When Hobbes wrote about what men are like by nature he was writing about how men actually behave, or how he thought they would actually behave. When Locke wrote about what men are like by nature he was writing about how men ought to behave, or how he thought they ought to behave. We sometimes blame on 'nature' our failure to reach the highest moral standards. 'It's only natural', people say, dismissing some fault as not worth taking seriously. (Similarly: 'He's only human'.) Sometimes, however, by contrast, we make an appeal to 'nature' when we want to stress the importance of high standards. What is in this sense 'natural' to man, meaning what is appropriate to human nature, is conduct on a rather high level. What men are like by nature can mean what men are ideally like. 'Realize true human nature', used to be said. Human beings have frequently been pictured as occupying a status midway between gods and beasts. In terms of this picture, Hobbes might be said to be looking down and Locke to be looking up. What is 'natural' to man, according to Hobbes, is to fall below this midway position. What is 'natural' to man, according to Locke, is to rise above it. But they are not understanding 'natural' in the same way; the area of disagreement between them is not as great as may appear. Locke is not altogether denying what Hobbes asserts, though he himself prefers not to assert it. Men, while they are by nature (that is, ideally) moral, cannot be relied upon in practice to avoid inroads upon each others' rights. Hence the need for political society — an artificial creation set up for the protection of the rights of individuals.

It is important not to see the wrong sort of significance in the individualism of such seventeenth century writers as Hobbes and Locke. In particular, their individualism does not prevent us calling them social philosophers. An individualist is not precluded from having views about society. Individualism is a kind of social philosophy, not a denial of it. It is not an obstacle in the way of social philosophy as it is in that of social science. Nevertheless, individualism leads to an impoverished kind of social philosophy and one which is constantly likely to misinterpret the relation between man and society. If we want to know what social philosophy is about we might do better to examine what the Greek philosophers said about society. Equally well we could look for illumination to writers of more recent times — for instance, to Hegel — for the Greeks are not the only social philosophers whose view of man in society has been non-individualistic in one way or another. But, generally speaking, such writers have learnt from the Greeks (this is certainly true of Hegel himself), and we may well think it preferable to turn to the masters rather than the pupils.

The Greek philosophers differed among themselves in what they had to say about society. The Sophists were interested in society because they were interested in social success. In order to get on well in a given society it is necessary to understand how that society works. The successful man needs to be able to persuade other men, and in order to persuade them he needs to understand what sort of men they are — in particular, what sort of things they value. We may confidently vote as most likely to succeed the man who has taken pains to adopt and manipulate the conventions of his society. The outsider is not a social success: this is a matter of definition. The conformist may be. The Sophists set themselves up as professional guidance counsellors in the business of getting on in society.

Socrates's interest in society went deeper. He wanted to investigate social concepts not as a means to social success (though he thought that virtue was teachable), but in order to make men question their beliefs — not necessarily as a preliminary to abondoning them but rather thereby to understand them better. Admittedly, Socrates was a somewhat ambiguous enemy of complacency. The Socrates presented in Plato's dialogues can sometimes irritate the reader with the apparently too-easy methods that he used to deflate his interlocutors. But Socrates introduced into philosophy a really serious study of questions like 'What is friendship?' (in the *Lysis*), 'What is courage?' (*Laches*), 'What is piety?' (*Euthyphro*), 'What is justice?' (*Republic*, Book I), and the clear recognition that the answering of such questions involves the close examination of social conventions.

Plato, in the *Republic*, demonstrates his interest as being that of a man who wanted to change society. Dissatisfaction with the state of affairs in an Athens which was capable of putting his revered teacher Socrates to death contributed to his theoretical devising of a better state of things. The main feature of the social ideal of the *Republic* are well known. Extreme democracy is bad; for the ignorant masses are incapable of governing themselves. Government ought to be in the hands of an intellectual elite — philosopher-kings. The rulers, or guardians, are to have property and wives in common (and their children are to be brought up apart, by the State), so that they will be distracted neither by avarice nor by family worries from the pursuit of the good and the government of the State. How this is to be achieved — at least as far as the education of the guardians is concerned — is described by Plato in detail. The fact remains that this is theory. Marx's dictum — 'The philosophers have only *interpreted* the world, in various ways; the point, however, is to *change* it' — may well seem to apply to Plato; for Plato's rebuilding of society was in the mind (though it would be unfair to say that he was not aware of the importance of testing theory against the realities of practice). The construction of utopias is a version of the interpretation of society, presented in the guise of changing it. Further, change, in this sphere as much as in any other, takes place against a background of permanence. The form a utopia assumes in its inventor's mind is determined by the society in which he himself lives, as well as, with the passage of time, by the influence of other literary examples. Whether improvement is to be effected by piecemeal social engineering (to use Sir Karl Popper's expression) or by a wholesale standing of a society upon its head, the ideal States that some philosophers have conceived it to be their duty to assist into the world of letters are tied by an umbilical cord to the societies that have given them birth. This is certainly the case with Plato.

Aristotle shared with Socrates and Plato an interest in the meaning of social and moral concepts — he discussed courage, liberality, 'magnanimity' or 'great-souledness', justice, friendship, and others — and he shared, too, an appreciation of the social implications of the moral virtues. Like Plato, Aristotle saw the good as no mere reflection of subjective opinion, but it is clear that he was interested in Greek virtues rather than in virtues of mankind in general. It is now that something like an empirical approach is made to the study of society. To the Socratic-Platonic mixture Aristotle added something not clearly present before his time: a strong interest in searching out facts — information on how different societies actually function. He, or others under his instruction, made a collection of 158 Constitutions — unfortunately now lost, except for that of Athens. Aristotle's empirical interests may tempt some to suppose they glimpse in his work an approximation to a social *science.* However, Aristotle was still, as Aquinas was to call him, The Philosopher. His interest, like Plato's, was in the last resort a philosophical interest in the ideal life. He did not even differ much from Plato in his view of what this life consists in: it is still, not surprisingly perhaps, the life of the philosopher; though for Aristotle pure contemplation rather than the mixed life of contemplation and ruling of the *Republic* represented the ultimate. If there is anything in the popular view of philosophers as mere theoreticians, or unpractical people, then Aristotle is as good a source for it as Plato.

From this brief account of the Greeks there emerges some kind of picture of what social philosophy is. First, the social philosopher studies social concepts. Emphases have changed, as societies have changed. Some of the concepts that particularly interested the Greeks — like courage or love — have been displaced from the foregound of interest by others — like authority or liberty. By no means all is changed, however. What Aristotle had to say about justice and about decision or choice is important and illuminating today. The essential point, however, is that no matter how much the emphasis may vary as between one age and another, one thing that makes and keeps a man a social philosopher is his involvement in the task of making social concepts clear — of defining them, of comparing one view about them with another. The concepts that seem important change from time to time. In other words, the subject matter of social philosophy changes from time to time. But its methods — basically those used in definition of concepts — have maintained a fair degree of continuity since the time of the Greeks. To take a topic that has been much discussed in recent years, that of punishment: the philosopher is interested in defining the concept of punishment and in assessing the theories that have been offered in justification of the infliction of punishment. It is clear that empirical evidence is not irrelevant to this interest. This is, indeed, a topic on which the social scientist and the social philosopher have much to give each other. The philosopher's interest here is basically a conceptual one; for instance, the question whether punishment is or is not in practice an effective deterrent is not strictly a philosophical question. But an adequate study of punishment must combine conceptual clarification (philosophy) with empircal investigation (science).

A second point that emerges concerns the interest of Plato in the construction of an ideal society. Not all later philosophers have shared this interest, but enough have done so to make it a characteristic of social philosophy. Philosophers have in general refrained from constructing ideal societies of the complexity of Plato's. But they have often been inspired in what they have written by some sort of vision of better things. Understanding purely for its own sake is a rarer thing than some would like to think it. Marx was not altogether fair to the philosophers. Hobbes, Locke, Rousseau, Mill — none of these wrote about society in the hope that their account of it should leave everything exactly as it was before. Theoretical writing, like that of Marx himself, can help to bring about changes in society. The contrast between understanding society and changing it is not a completely-sharp one. No one can change a society who does not first understand it; and those understand it best who bring to it a concern with both facts and values.

We have noted the interest of the Greeks in the social conventions of their own and of other societies; and along with this goes an interest in the question of whether all social conventions and rules are *merely* conventional, or whether some of them have some 'objective' basis. This interest in 'nature versus convention' and in the character of social rules — moral and political rules in particular — is a third feature of social philosophy where the Greeks represent only the beginning of a continuing tradition.

There is a fourth feature to be added to these three, though to find it we must look elsewhere than to the Greeks. Philosophy, although itself a special study, also stands in a unique relationship to other special studies. Consider the way in which the word 'philosophy' is linked with the names of other studies in the expression 'the philosophy of . . .': the philosophy of history, the philosophy of religion, the philosophy of law, the philosophy of the natural sciences, the philosophy of the social sciences. It is the last-mentioned that concerns us here. One of the prime concerns of philosophers is with the methods used in, and, indeed, with the whole nature and aims of, other studies. The practice of the scientist, the historian, the lawyer, gives rise to questions of a methodological kind and to questions about aims. Such questions may not always occur to scientists, historians, or lawyers themselves. But if they do pursue them, they are engaged in philosophizing about their own subject rather than in directly doing it. This kind of self-consciousness in regard to one's subject can be as much of a hindrance as a help — as paying too close attention to the movements of your legs in walking can trip you up. Many successful scientists have never bothered with the questions of what science is really about and what science is for; and some of those who have been seriously concerned with such questions have been indifferent scientists. Nevertheless, these questions will go on being asked. There is probably more advantage than disadvantage to practical science from asking them: but even if this were not so, it is right that they should be asked. No investigation that carries further the process of understanding the pursuits of men can be other than intellectually worth while — whether it has obvious 'practical' use or not. Indeed, the questions of what practical usefulness is, and how its value is to be assessed, are themselves questions of this fundamental kind; they are not easy to answer, but they cannot be avoided.

Questions about the methods and aims of the social sciences are philosophical questions. The methodology (or philosophy) of the social sciences is a branch of philosophy, whether undertaken by professional philosophers or by social scientists themselves. Philosophers have never claimed proprietary rights in the name of their own subject. Naturally, where methodology is done by professional philosophers it is as well if they know something at first hand about the social sciences: equally, where it is done by social scientists it is as well if they in their turn know something about philosophy.

Strictly speaking, the philosophy of the social sciences needs to be distinguished from social philosophy proper. There is a difference between the first-order activity of philosophizing about society and the second-order activity of philosophizing about the scientific study of society. Nevertheless, in an extended sense of 'social philosophy' we may say that it includes some study of the methods of social science. The philosopher is interested both in society and in the ways in which men have tried to describe and explain society. It is difficult to keep these two interests apart. Indeed, it is doubtful whether they ought to be kept apart. Our understanding of society is determined by, among other things, the methods that we bring to its investigation. An acute awareness of his own methods is a mark of the philosopher, especially of the contemporary philosopher; and the social philosopher cannot understand his own methods unless he understands them in relation to those of the social scientist.

Interest in society is, of course, not limited to social philosophers and social scientists. The dramatist and the novelist have their own contributions to make to our understanding of society. There are writers who combine several talents: scientist-philosophers and novelist-dramatist-philosophers.

The novelist or dramatist is interested in individuals and the forces that work upon individuals. He may illuminate the society to which his characters belong, as did Galsworthy, or Trollope; or by implication some other society, as does William Golding in *Lord of the Flies*: indeed, to shed light upon society may even be a prime intention of his writing (*Gulliver's Travels*; some of H. G. Wells). But his method is to proceed not by generalizing about human nature but by creating individuals whose identity as individuals and whose relations to other individuals are essential to the piece of writing that he is engaged in. It is commonly said that the philosopher (even where he is an individualist) and the scientist are interested not in the concrete but in the general, in the sense that they are interested not in *specific* individuals but in human nature or in the character of a given society. However, social scientists sometimes proceed by telling stories about specific individuals (case histories) and often draw no explicitly general conclusions from them. Philosophers, too, on occasion have told stories about individuals (for example, the myths in Plato's *Republic*), though they generally find it harder than the scientists to refrain from pointing morals; it would be difficult to deny altogether the name of philosophy to Sartre's novels and plays and to insist on reserving it for his more obviously abstract writings. And what of novels which tell no stories? Now novels and plays, generally speaking, are fiction; the social scientists' case histories are fact. Yet there are novels and plays which tell true stories. Further, the line between some journalism and some social science is often claimed, with justice, to be hard to draw.

So there are 'stories' both in literature and in philosophy and science. Perhaps so, the reader may say; but there are *theories* only in philosophy and science. Not at all. Admittedly, when there are theories about society or morals or history in a play, we can try to see them as part of the presentation of individual character, although this is not easy to do in the case of Shaw; and when there are such theories in a novel — for example, *War and Peace* — we can try to see them as extraneous to 'the novel itself', though we should surely be wrong in doing this, to the extent that the novel is a unity or a successful work of art. The truth is that a severe compartmentalization is not always possible. Probably it is not always advisable. We can learn from anything. If our interest is in man and society, then illumination from any source is welcome — literature, journalism, philosophy, science, or any other. These differ in their methods. They need not differ so much in their end: the better understanding of man.

Let us return to the question of the relation between social science and social philosophy. As far as the contribution of philosophy is concerned the first element is an historical one. As we have noted, it was the Greek philosophers who began the study of society. They were not social scientists, but in a real sense social science may be said to have grown out of their, and subsequent, philosophy. For that matter, all the sciences grew out of philosophy; the only difference in the case of social science was that it took longer. Without a beginning there can be no development, no radical changes of direction, nothing. It was philosophers who nursed through their infancy what were, or were to become, the social sciences. They were not always good influences, but if it had not been for philosophers these subjects might not have progressed at all. Consider the place of Adam Smith and Mill in economics, Marx in sociology and in politics, James in psychology. (Marx we may allow to have begun as a philosopher and James to have ended as one.)

The contribution that philosophy can make is a varied one. The value of conceptual clarity cannot be overstated. Concepts like those of authority, responsibility, motive, fact and value, are essentially involved in the study of society. Empirical investigation without conceptual clarity is worthless. The former interest of philosophers in the theoretical construction of ideal societies has less to commend it; but even this could be of value to the extent that, as we noted, the pursuit of ideals can be an indirect way of illuminating realities — though indirection is not usually accounted a virtue by scientists. The value of the work done by philosophers on the methodology of the social sciences needs no emphasis, nor does that of their work on the nature of social rules.

The social scientist is probably readier to acknowledge that philosophy can be of use to him than the philosopher is to acknowledge the reverse. The social sciences nowadays give the philosopher material to work on. That he too often does not take advantage of it is nobody's fault but his own. The philosopher can better achieve clarity about social concepts if he knows some *facts* about society (not that social science limits itself to the providing of facts).

The social scientist and the social philosopher have much to give each other, much to learn from each other. However, a warning must be entered here. It would be wrong to look on their relation as one of superiority and inferiority − in either direction. Neither is the servant of the other, and the use of the terminology of 'contributing to' is not intended to suggest this. Indeed, to avoid misunderstanding, it might be better not to think in terms of what the philosopher can do for the social scientist or he for the philosopher. The point is rather that above science and philosophy there is something more general than either − the overall enterprise of understanding man in society. It is to this overall enterprise that science and philosophy together contribute, rather than either to the other.

What is it to understand man in society? What society? Machiavelli's understanding of his society is different from Marx's understanding of his; and different for the reason, among others, that the two men lived in very different times. In so far as their interest − *pace* Marx − has been practical, philosophers have tried to write both with the aim of explaining the circumstances and answering the needs of their own times and also, more importantly, with that of offering a diagnosis of, and a cure for, social ills that will be valid for the future. We should not call them philosophers at all if they stopped short at the first task − and indeed on these grounds it is doubtful how far Machiavelli ought to be called a philosopher. A balance between these two aims is difficult to strike. The first can influence the second; and ought to, if the philosopher is not to drift off into the abstract. Social philosophers have wanted to understand society, where social scientists tend to be content with understanding societies; but the philosophers have generally been perfectly well aware that society is an abstraction from societies.

Social philosophy, like social science, no doubt needs to be done over again in every age; but social philosophers, unlike social scientists, constantly look back to the work of their predecessors and find in it new starting points. A fair amount of what Plato or Hobbes or Rousseau said applies to our condition, even if hardly any of it applies directly. The opinions of the philosophers of the past about man and society are not always worth more than those of other people — though they are not worth any less. But it is not their mere opinions that later philosophers find illuminating; it is rather their arguments and the help they provide towards the clarification of concepts. That Hobbes thought men fearful by nature is interesting, but a man does not have to be a philosopher to hold an opinion like that. What is of more interest in Hobbes is his arguments based upon this opinion — arguments concerning what, assuming that men are fearful by nature, may be supposed to follow from this — and the way in which in the course of his discussion he throws light upon notions like those of obligation, sovereignty and punishment, notions which we are likely to need in any discussion of man in society. The social philosophy of the past is the foundation for that of today, even where that foundation is not explicitly uncovered.

CHAPTER 2

# Understanding Society

IN the previous chapter I uttered a warning against what might be called the 'hand-maiden' view: the view that the function of philosophy is that of helping on the work of science. Some philosophers have certainly taken something like a hand-maiden view of their subject; and some others, in reaction, have taken up a strongly contrary position.

Part of what is involved in the hand-maiden view (or the underlabourer view, as Professor Peter Winch has called it with reference to a passage in Locke's *Essay Concerning Human Understanding*) is a particular opinion about philosophy: namely, that philosophy does not give *knowledge* of society, whereas social science does. This, it is supposed, is because a society, to be properly understood, needs to be regarded as an object of study independent of the person studying it. The proper attitude to adopt towards it is assumed to be that of the dispassionate empirical investigator. The philosopher does not engage in empirical investigation; his task is that of the clarification of concepts. So we have a sharp division drawn between scientific, by which is understood empirical, investigation of society, and the useful ancillary, but non-empirical, work of the philosopher, which can be regarded as no more than a sharpening of conceptual tools for the scientist to use.

As against this it has been maintained that a society cannot be understood merely by being observed from the outside as an empirical object of study. Narrowly empirical methods are inadequate to the study of society. We cannot understand a society unless we understand what the people in it mean by the concepts they use; but no amount of purely empirical study can tell us this. The investigation of concepts is the philosopher's business. At the opposite extreme to the hand-maiden view would be the view that, far from its being the case that the philosopher can give us no understanding of society, *only* the philosopher, by his methods, can give us understanding, and the empirical scientist, by his, cannot. A purely empirical social science would be impossible in the sense that the aim of social science — the understanding of society — can never be achieved by purely empirical methods. If we want to understand a society we must be social philosophers, not social scientists: so this view would run.

This should not be confused with the milder view that because the social scientist is in the last resort studying people, there is an uncertainty about his material. People do unexpected things; they act out of character. Their behaviour is more difficult to predict than is that of, say, stars and planets, or even lions and foxes (for people have 'free will', whereas stars, planets, lions and foxes do not); for instance, the publishing of predictions of their behaviour can influence that behaviour in a contrary direction, as people who had not intended to vote for Harry Truman in the 1948 American Presidential elections nevertheless did so *because* the polls had predicted that people would not vote for him. This adds up to the view that empirical social science is exceedingly difficult. The claim of the view mentioned above, however, is the much more radical one that it is impossible.

As usual when one finds a conflict between extremes the truth lies somewhere in the middle. It can be shown that a narrowly empirical social science alone is not adequate to the explanation of society; but it certainly would not follow from this that social science is worthless and that philosophy must take its place. Both science and philosophy are needed: but what is needed also is an understanding of what each can do. One of my chief aims in this chapter is to bring out the inadequacy of a too narrowly empirical approach to the study of society. I shall be discussing the shortcomings of a *type* of approach, and it may well be that no one has advanced a view as crudely simple as that which I criticize (though I do not doubt that some have come close to it). But this does not matter. I am adopting a simple model of a type of inadequate explanation of society (the noise-and-movement type of 'explanation') in order; through criticism of it, to make some points about what is necessary for an adequate explanation of society.

A narrowly empirical study of a society cannot give us full understanding of that society. It is clear that we cannot understand a society simply by observing the movements through which its members go and the noises they make. We need to know what those movements and noises mean. A purely external empirical investigation alone cannot tell us this. Some understanding of the institutions and the concepts of the society is needed, and this is not possible unless in some sense we are inside the society.

Suppose an observer from Mars to be set down in modern Britain. If he adopts a narrowly empirical attitude the reports that he sends back to his headquarters will at the beginning be reports of movements and noises. But what do these movements and noises mean? He may impose his own pattern of meaning on them and this may satisfy him, but he has not yet understood the society he is studying. For that he must discover what those movements and noises mean to those who make them. Of course, the movements and noises are only the surface of the institutions that go to make up the society; the aspects of the life of a society, tangible and intangible, are multifarious. What are the buildings for? What rôle is played in the society by this person or that? The observer from Mars will need to find out something about the past of the society if he is to understand its present. He will also need to learn the language of the society, which may mean in effect learning several languages.

None of this is possible unless he brings to his task a highly complex conceptual apparatus. It goes without saying that he must know what a language is, otherwise the noises he hears uttered by the people around him will never suggest to him even the possibility that he ought to try to learn what they mean — any more than it occurs to us to try to find out what the noise of the wind in overhead telephone wires means. It goes without saying also that he must have at least the concept of society itself, otherwise the people that he sees and everything that he sees them doing will no more suggest to him any need for explanation in terms of meaningful behaviour than the movement of the grains of sand on the beach suggests this to us. That these things do have a meaning he must already be disposed to believe, otherwise the Martians have sent the wrong man. What they mean, however, will never reveal itself to him as long as he simply collects empirical data. He may interpret what he sees by analogy with Martian society, and this may or may not come close to the truth. Perhaps in the end this will be the best he can do. We can only understand what we can fit into familiar categories. But supposing Martian categories to be very different from ours, would we not say that the Martian observer when he departs takes away something that he thinks is understanding, whereas he has not really understood the society at all? Of course, there are degrees of understanding, and the Martian is an extreme case. But social anthropologists and other students of societies can still fail to understand if they adopt too much of the Martian approach. What is needed is the attitude of the insider, not that of the unengaged on-looker; and an interest in social concepts, not just in observable behaviour.

The shortcomings of a narrowly empirical study of society have been forcefully presented by a number of philosophers in recent years – notably by Professor Winch, following Wittgenstein. There are several elements in recent philosophical criticism of a narrowly empirical social science and these are intimately related to each other; but we can for purposes of discussion isolate three of them. First, there is the stress, already mentioned, on the need to see things from the inside, not from the outside. Secondly, a contrast is drawn between explanation in terms of causes (which is the kind of explanation the scientist offers) and explanation in terms of reasons, and the claim is made that in the study of society the former is inadequate. Thirdly, there is a stress on the notion of 'meaningfulness' in social behaviour (this also has been touched upon) – in particular a stress on rule-following.

No one can begin to understand a society who does not see it as far as is possible for him 'from the inside'. But it must be a rather special kind of seeing from the inside: the adoption of an attitude of sympathy is not enough. The Martian no doubt will strive hard to 'feel with' the people he is studying, but this may not help him. It is not a matter of the will. We must be as far as possible one with the society we are studying, but the connexion between seeing from the inside and understanding is a logical rather than an empirical one. It is sometimes claimed that understanding logically involves sharing the conceptual scheme of the society we are studying, so that anything that did not involve this could not properly be *called* understanding.

Only the Martian, as I have already hinted, is likely to find himself completely on the outside. Our own social scientists do, as a matter of fact, share a large part of the conceptual scheme of the people they study. What they are studying is fellow human beings, and however much societies and institutions may differ there is always much in which they do not differ. The possession of language, in particular, is something in common as between different periods and places — not the possession of the same language, obviously, but the possession of some system of communication of complex conceptual matters. A distinguished physicist has remarked that in a sense a child of three already knows more physics than he will ever learn even if he grows up to be a specialist in the subject. Equally, we might say that a child of three already knows more about society than he will ever learn even if he grows up to become a social scientist. The child is on the inside of society: he has acquired language, and in acquiring language he has acquired a basic acquaintance with what living in society means; he is well on the way to building on this an understanding of other societies than his own.

The fact, then, that societies can only be understood from the inside is not one that places an insuperable difficulty in the way of the social scientist (though it does place an insuperable difficulty in the way of a purely noise-and-movement social scientist). He cannot help, on one level, seeing things from the inside. He is inside social life. Of course, there are degrees of inside-ness. The middle-class student social worker, engaged in practical work in the slums of her city, may say, 'I shall never understand these people.' A complacent student social anthropologist may suppose that he understands pretty well the primitive people among whom he is doing his field work. Probably in fact the social worker understands much better than the anthropologist: the points of contact are obscured by differences that are — relatively speaking — trivial. The anthropologist, whatever he may himself suppose, is probably much nearer to the situation of the observer from Mars than is the social worker. Older-fashioned anthropologists used to adopt a more stand-offish attitude than do anthropologists today. To a certain degree, however, both the old-fashioned and the new-fashioned are looking from the inside, in a way that someone altogether outside human society — if we can conceive of such — never could.

It is true that the approach of the scientist is determined by his possession of a certain conceptual scheme, which may not be the same as the conceptual scheme of the people or the institutions that he is studying. But neither is it totally different. On a very basic level he is bound to share certain concepts with the people he is studying. He cannot be literally in the position of a *total* outsider. As we have already noted, if he is a social being, let alone a social scientist, he must know what a society is, and there are other concepts that he must have as well. Without them it would not even make sense to suppose him a 'social scientist'.

The danger of his misunderstanding what he is studying, through imposing on what he sees an interpretation determined by the concepts of his own society, is a real one. But he must resist it, and there is no reason why he should not be able to resist it. What is needed is a recognition by the social scientist that seeing from the inside and not merely from the outside is necessary for the understanding of a society. It is not the case, then, that social scientists cannot understand societies but rather that if they limit themselves to a narrowly empirical approach they cannot. Mere reporting of noises and movements would not constitute any kind of serious scientific study of society. To have the concept of society at all and to know that one is a human being studying human beings, not sticks and stones, is to be in some degree on the inside. A social scientist who believed himself a mere noise-and-movement man would be mistaken. His practice cannot be that of a mere noise-and-movement man, even if he should happen to hold a theory that says that noises and movements are all that the social scientist can study. No social scientist can help being to some extent on the inside; the attitude of the complete outsider is impossible for anyone who has, as we might say, passed the age of three in human society. Noise-and-movement social scientists would not be the first people to misunderstand the nature of their own subject and to misunderstand what they themselves are engaged in.

We pass now to the contrast between explanation in terms of causes and explanation in terms of reasons. Suppose someone were to take his own life. We can give a causal explanation of his death, in the sense that we can account for it in terms of, say, the effect on his body of a fall from a height on to a hard surface. But such an explanation does not enable us to distinguish between the case of the man who falls off a cliff because he trips or is pushed and that of the man who jumps off because he has been jilted. The description of an action as one of 'taking his own life' presupposes that alongside the question of how he died is that of why he died – we are interested not in the cause of his death but in the reason for his suicide. This latter question expects an answer using expressions like 'depression', 'jilted', 'knowledge of an incurable disease'.

The contrast between causes and reasons, as represented by this example, is not an entirely sharp one as far as terminology is concerned. Though we should probably not speak of something like a fall from a height, or poison, or water in the lungs, as 'reasons' for death, we do sometimes speak of depression, jilting, inoperable cancer, as 'causes' of suicide. But however we choose to express it the contrast itself is a real one, and the words 'reason' and 'cause' point it well enough. When we are dealing with things that human beings do, whether as individuals or in society, explanation in terms of reasons as well as causes is needed for completeness. A social scientist who confined himself to causes would be giving some kind of explanation of human behaviour, but it would often be an incomplete explanation.

Here again the work of the philosopher has the effect of providing methodological clarity. But, of course, to say that there is need for explanation of human behaviour in terms of reasons is certainly not to say that only the philosopher can adequately explain human behaviour. A narrowly empirical social science (confining itself to causes and neglecting reasons) would be mistaken; but to recognize this is not to say that only social philosophy and not social science can really explain human behaviour. The philosopher stresses the importance of looking for reasons; but he is in no specially privileged position as far as the discovery of reasons is concerned. The methods of the social scientist are still appropriate here. What the scientist must avoid is the refusal of interest in reasons, but granted that he avoids this his methods (of observation) can be used in their discovery.

The third matter to be discussed is the importance of the notions of meaningfulness and rule-following. Meaningful action has sometimes been identified with rule-governed action. This may be more fully explained by reference to the question, a good deal discussed in recent philosophy, of the possibility of a private language (see Winch, (1) pp. 24–39). Consider what would be involved in the existence of a purely private language. We may suppose an imaginary inventor of a private language to make a certain noise when a bird of a particular shape and colouring passes overhead and to decide that thereafter he will make the same noise whenever such a bird passes again. This, we must suppose, is to be a purely private arrangement. There is never anyone else nearby to hear the noise; or, if we like, we may suppose that he makes the noise in his head and not out loud, or that it is not a case of making a noise at all but rather of making a particular kind of scratch on the rocks in a place where no one else could possibly see it. (It is part of the definition of 'private language' in this sense that no one else is ever involved, whether at the time or subsequently. If anyone else were to come to share the language it would no longer be, in the sense required, a private language. The sense of private language here is that of a language inescapably private or private by definition; not that of a language that happens to be private but that in principle could be understood by others — for instance, a code in which a private diary is kept.) We are to suppose, that is to say, that our inventor of a private language creates a rule that he will make the same noise or the same mark whenever a bird of the same kind flies over; and this will be a primitive private language.

Wittgenstein, and following him Winch and others, argue, however, that this supposition is meaningless. One of their chief arguments against it is that in these circumstances it is impossible to give any meaning to the notion of making a mistake in the following of a rule and consequently impossible to give any meaning to that of following a rule. The point being made here is the following. There can be no difference between a correct and an incorrect use of a private language. In a private language, supposing there to be such a thing, there would be no way of distinguishing between following a rule and merely thinking that one was following a rule. How would one know if one had made a mistake in the use of one's words? What is there to appeal to that would settle a question like that? Other people's uses are, *ex hypothesi*, not available. One cannot appeal to memory; for how could one know if one was remembering correctly? In short, if using a language involves following rules, as it does, there can be no such thing as an inescapably private language; for if there is no way of telling when one is following a rule correctly and when one is making a mistake, then there is no meaning to the notion of following a rule. One way in which this argument is developed concerns the notion of *the same*. It is claimed that the user of a purely private language could

not have this notion. Professor Norman Malcolm writes: 'The point
to be made here is that when one has given oneself the private rule
"I will call this same thing 'pain' whenever it occurs", one is then free
to do anything or nothing. That "rule" does not point in any direction. On the private-language hypothesis, no one can teach me what
the correct use of "same" is. I shall be the sole arbitor of whether
this is the *same* as that. What I choose to call the "same" will *be* the
same. No restriction whatever will be imposed upon my application
of the word. But a sound that I can use *as I please* is not a *word*'
(Malcolm, p.103).

We cannot understand a society unless we are able to see the *meaning* of what its members do — and see the meaning as they see it. This
is a truism. One important aspect of this is that we have to understand the *rules* that they follow in what they do. The controversy
about the possibility of a private language is a controversy about
whether rules — here considered in the particular case of rules of
language — are or are not dependent upon social existence. The
Wittgensteinian view is that they are. The critics of this view (including Professor A. J. Ayer and Professor P. F. Strawson) in maintaining
the possibility of a private language, are maintaining that rules — at
any rate in the case of the rules of a language — are not dependent upon
social existence. The issue here is one of whether the notion of meaningful behaviour, or rule-governed behaviour, is socially dependent. It
is not relevant to our present purpose to enter further into the private
language controversy. For the present I shall make only the following
comment: given that there is a society it is certainly true that there
must be discoverable in it rule-governed behaviour. The notions of
'meaningful' behaviour or 'rule-governed' behaviour (or rather action)
are of the greatest importance in the understanding of society; and
recent philosophical discussion has served to bring out sharply the
inadequacy of a narrowly empirical approach in the handling of these
notions.

There is another kind of objection that can be brought against
a narrowly empirical social science, or a behaviouristic noise-and-
movement approach. This approach is closely associated with the
inductivist attitude to science; and to the extent that there are faults in
inductivism there are consequently faults in the noise-and-movement
school in social science. Inductivism is that view of scientific method

that sees the scientist as a passive observer of 'facts', who goes on observing until out of the facts emerges in some logical way the theory that is going to explain these facts; the ideal of inductivism is that there should be no interpretation of the facts in the light of an already-held theory.

It has been argued by Sir Karl Popper that inductivism offers an inadequate account of how the scientific enterprise is carried on (Popper (1), (2)), though it has been supposed by some that the success of science was due largely to its patient waiting upon facts. No amount of staring at 'facts' will bring forth an explanatory theory. We must at least have some idea of what we are looking for if we are to have any chance of finding it. Induction (argument from the particular to the general) is difficult to reduce to rules, though logicians have tried to do it: this difficulty itself suggests that there is something odd about the inductivist view of scientific method. Popper rejects the notion of a *logic* of induction, the notion that induction is a separate variety of reasoning, which can be summed up in a set of rules. 'Induction' is rather another name for guessing or leaping in the dark, something that by its very nature cannot be described in terms of rules and regularities. The scientist, immersed in certain facts and deeply concerned with some problem, has a flash of inspiration. This is a hypothesis, or conjecture, about the explanation of the facts or the answer to the problem. It is claimed that it is not possible to give an account of the process by which he arrives at his hypothesis; there is no process, in the sense that there are no distinguishable steps of reasoning through which he has gone and which could be neatly tabulated. An idea about how his problem might be solved — a hunch — has come to him: it does not matter how it has come or from where. The important question is whether it succeeds as a solution. For this, procedures of testing must be gone through. These can be reduced to rules, although the original arriving at the presumed solution cannot. Hence the use of the expressions 'hypothetico-deductive' and 'conjecture-refutation', as descriptions of the method of the scientist according to Popper. A hypothesis or conjecture having — no matter how — appeared, the scientist deduces what ought to be the case if that hypothesis were correct, and then observes or experiments to see whether it is in fact the case. If it is, so far so good; the hypothesis is not yet refuted. If it is not the case, the hypothesis must be abandoned, and the scientist must wait for another before going through the process of testing all over again. The scientist does use logic, but Popper claims that inductivists are wrong in thinking that there is a special kind of logic — inductive logic — used typically by scientists (though not by them alone). There is only one kind of logic available to the scientist as to everybody else: deductive logic. The point at which logic comes into science is not, as the inductivists suppose, in the arriving at scientific theories, hypotheses, generalizations, or conjectures, but in the testing of these. Testing, furthermore, must always be undertaken in the hope of refutation, not of confirmation. Indeed, it is impossible for any scientific theory ever to be finally and conclusively confirmed. There must always remain the possibility of its being overthrown, however unlikely we may want to believe this to be. To suppose otherwise is to be untrue to the spirit of the scientific enterprise, and in any case is impossible, for if we did ever arrive at the final truth we should have no way of knowing that it was the final truth. Science advances to the extent that scientists never rest content with what they have got. Their attitude to their theories should be that of the doubting prosecutor, not that of the doting parent who refuses to see the faults in his child. Scientists are as likely as anyone else to fall short of their ideal, but the progress of science depends upon their not falling short of it too often.

Popper's account of science is based in the first instance on physics, but it has been extended much more widely both by himself and by others. It has been extended, indeed, outside science altogether, and the conjecture-refutation pattern has been used in the study of politics, aesthetics, religion and philosophy. Its usefulness to the social scientist is considerable.

As we have noted, the reasoned rejection of inductivism offers ammunition to fire at the noise-and-movement school in social science. To the extent that social scientists have supposed themselves able to understand society purely through the collection and examination of observable facts about societies, they need to consider Popper's charge that this is not the method of science.

Further, this approach offers an antidote to possible despair. If the task of the social scientist were indeed simply to sit down before the facts and wait for them to speak to him, his could be a frustrating task. Waiting for someone who may never come, or who if he comes may not speak, or if he speaks may not speak sense, is not a task to be wished on anybody. But if this view is right, the scientist has something to do. The scientific enterprise is active, not passive (and it is not active merely in the sense that the scientist may be busily occupied in gathering facts). There is no need to wait upon the facts and perhaps wait for ever. The scientist wants not just facts but answers; there are only answers where there are questions; and questions are put by inquiring minds. It is the scientist who calls the tune, not the 'facts'. Of course, social scientists do not actually suffer from the despair of blankness, and this may be an indication that Popper's view is not merely useful but (in part anyway) correct.

There is also an associated stress in this view on the social or co-operative character of science. It is part of the nature of the scientific enterprise that it should be carried on in the open. There is never any need to justify the publication of scientific results; there is always need to justify their suppression. It is because it is necessary for the advance of science that conjectures should be tested that it is necessary for them to be published. A scientist's rivals are more likely than he is himself to enter with enthusiasm into the task of overthrowing his theories. Popper's insistence on falsification, on the search for the instances that may refute a conjecture, has as its corollary an insistence on the public character of science. Many heads are better than one, and some knives are sharper than others. No creation without co-operation; and in science rivalry is a form of co-operation. This is an ideal picture, no doubt, but the encouragement it gives to the scientist, including the social scientist, is considerable.

We need also to note Popper's anti-historicism (Popper (3), (4)). There is no finality in science, and there is no ultimate clue to the understanding of human behaviour or the course of human history. It is false to believe that examination of the facts of history will reveal general laws of history that can be used to predict the future (the belief that there are such laws is what Popper calls historicism, and he finds it in Plato, Aristotle, Hegel and Marx). There are no laws to be discovered from recurring patterns in history. To understand human life we must take it as it is, and not suppose that there is some clue to history that will explain what it is all about and tell us in advance what is going to happen. The Spenglers and Toynbees are mistaken. The objection is not to the historian's approaching his

C

documents, or whatever his material may be, with an already-formed theory; in this respect the historian uses methods of conjecture and refutation parallel to those of the scientist. The objection is to the procedure of thinkers who suppose that history exhibits the working of some Grand Plan, and that when we have somehow discovered what this is we can predict man's future. This serves as a warning against the devising of overall explanatory hypotheses in social science that are supposed to give understanding of human-nature-in-general or society-in-general. These would not be scientific theories at all. The behaviour of human beings in society does not lend itself to explanation and prediction in terms of grand laws like the 'laws of (physical) nature' that our forefathers spoke of.

Popper's attack on historicism is inspired by a belief that it is associated with practical political and social developments. In Plato he sees the ultimate inspirer of modern totalitarianism. This connexion, supposing it to be true, would certainly not render his view less urgent or important. In general, a readiness to connect theory and practice is no disrecommendation of any view that bears on social science. Yet another respect in which Popper's ideas are of value to the social scientist, is, indeed, that of their practical bearing. Following on the rejection of historicism is the recommendation of the method of 'piecemeal social engineering'. If there are no grand laws of history then utopian schemes, based on beliefs about allegedly permanent aspects of human nature, are of no practical worth. If society is to be changed it must be changed bit by bit. In terms of practical politics socialism is to be rejected in favour of something like the liberalism of theorists like Locke or Mill, or, to come to our own day, Michael Oakeshott. Overall planning must give way to particular small-scale changes.

This perhaps needs qualification. If we reject the belief in laws of history we are not bound to move straight to a belief that overall social planning is impossible, and it is not a necessary condition of adherence to overall social planning that one should also adhere to a belief in inexorable laws of history. We may grant that there are no laws on the basis of which the future can be surely predicted. Men make their own future. But they can make their own future either piecemeal or in accordance with a general plan. As Popper has pointed out, the very existence of a plan can itself alter the future in such a way that the plan no longer fits and we need another one, but this is neither more nor less true than that piecemeal social engineering can create conditions that call for more piecemeal social engineering. It is not obvious (the alleged connexion with features of Nazism and Communism apart) that a general plan is worse than piecemeal social engineering.

Popper's rejection of a logic of induction is whole-hearted, but perhaps too whole-hearted: a lack of interest in how a generalization is arrived at by the scientist involves turning one's back on details and differences that might well be significant. It is illuminating to present Galileo, Newton, Darwin, Freud or Einstein as men who had hunches, or who leapt in the dark. But how did they come to find themselves leaping? In what circumstances did such-and-such a hunch occur? Information of this kind can be of more than merely biographical interest; it can also be of interest to a student of creativity in science or elsewhere. Some of this curiosity, admittedly, is on a level with that of the dull student who plies the distinguished visiting speaker with polite questions about how many hours a day he devotes to his work, what time he goes to bed, whether he recommends taking full notes or few, or approves of reading many books once only or a few many times — as if there were rules which if faithfully followed would be sure to lead to success in science or scholarship. But without committing oneself to a belief in clear rules of discovery there is still more to be said about what goes on than that it is (in effect) a matter of fortunate guesses. There *is* a logic of induction. Argument from the particular to the general can be either well-founded or ill-founded. We distinguish good inductive arguments from bad inductive arguments (see Strawson, (1), pp. 244—8), and unless we are deceiving ourselves when we make this distinction there must be rules of some kind involved in the making of it. It is not irrelevant in the assessing of an inductive argument to consider questions like the method of sampling used and the evidence for causal connexions between the items related. To say this is already to have said that there is a kind of *logic* of inductive reasoning.

To say that science never reaches finality is true, but is open to the objection that it may obscure the special character that some scientific hypotheses have attained. The Newtonian 'laws' of motion or the 'laws' of evolution are by now incapable of being overthrown without the collapse of the very sciences built up around them. These are hardly to be described as hypotheses or conjectures. Such 'laws' set the limits, define the subject matter, within which scientific hypothesizing or conjecturing can take place. Scientific theories exist on different levels; and the notion of continuous progress by means of conjecture and refutation makes better sense on the lower levels than on the higher. But there is certainly great virtue in the view of science as constantly open to correction, and as far as a new field like social science is concerned the notion that there is neither certainty nor finality is of particular value. The acceptance of this insistence on lack of finality means that we may hope to avoid the mistake of stopping too soon — of thinking that we have reached in social science the equivalent of Newton's laws of motion. Social science is short on theory, but even so it is better that what theories there are should be of a limited character. Finality, which is not always easily distinguishable from death, may well be done without.

Winch and Popper represent points of view which are in some respects opposed to each other, but together their significance for the social scientist is considerable. Winch himself has repudiated the suggestion that he is writing with methodological intent (Winch (1) p.36; (2)), but it is nevertheless possible to interpret some of his ideas as being concerned with methodology. Popper's certainly are. The foregoing discussion, as will be entirely obvious, has been conducted in a very general way. A main intention behind it has been to illustrate one aspect of social philosophy — that which I described in the previous chapter as methodological. The philosopher is interested in social science partly because he is interested in society but also because he is interested in the differences between other kinds of study and his own. The philosopher hopes to make clearer to the scientist what the nature of his (the scientist's) enterprise is. Sometimes he succeeds, sometimes he fails. The social scientist who listens to philosophers like Winch and Popper — though often they speak with contrary voices — may learn something about his own activity. At the same time, we need to remember the lesson that nothing is final, in science or in philosophy; and that includes the philosophy of the social sciences.

# CHAPTER 3

# Social Rules

LIFE in society is life governed by rules. The kinds of social rule that chiefly interest the social philosopher are moral, legal, and political rules. (There are, of course, many social rules that are neither moral, legal, nor political.) These rules reflect certain features of human nature. The views of human nature held by philosophers have been fairly varied (we shall return to this in a later chapter), but philosophers have on the whole not differed much in their views about the rules that have seemed to them to arise out of the nature and needs of man. That men are fearful of one another — as Hobbes supposed they were — requires that they submit to the restrictions of society for their own protection. That they are well-disposed to one another — as Locke thought they were, or at least ought to be — equally ensures that they live under social rules. That men live rule-governed lives follows from their living social lives at all, whether we suppose, with Hobbes, that men are social against their inclinations, or, with Locke, that they are social in accordance with them.

That social life is rule-governed will perhaps not be disputed. What is disputed, however, is whether or not there is some indispensable content to social rules. That is, can a society have any rules as long as it has some, or are there certain rules which any society must have? On the assumption that it is necessary to accept survival as an aim of man (for 'our concern is with social arrangements for continued existence, not with those of a suicide club'), Professor H.L.A. Hart has listed the following 'truisms' lying behind law and morality: (1) human vulnerability ('if men were to lose their vulnerability to each other there would vanish one obvious reason for the most characteristic provision of law and morals: *Thou shalt not kill.*'); (2) approximate equality ('no individual is so much more powerful than others, that he is able, without co-operation, to dominate or subdue them for more than a short period'); (3) limited altruism; (4) limited resources; and (5) limited understanding and strength of will (sanctions are needed to coerce those who may fail to see the advantages of conformity; they are 'a *guarantee* that those who would voluntarily obey shall not be sacrificed to those who would not'). (See Hart (2), pp. 188-195). Given that men live in society, and that they are vulnerable to attack from each other, are unlikely to get the upper hand over their fellows for long, are altruistic only up to a point, are in competition for limited resources, and are in need of protection from those who prefer the short-run advantage, it follows, according to Hart, that law and morality must have a definite content:  there must be rules providing for the protection of 'persons, property, and promises', and these rules must have sanctions attached to them. As long as 'human beings and the world they live in' retain the characteristics that they have, so long will rules of this kind be necessary.

The view that there are certain rules which any society must have is, then, maintained by Hart. The different view that a society can have any rules as long as it has some has been maintained by Lord Devlin. The debate between Devlin and Hart about the enforcement of morality has brought out this disagreement as a rather surprising side issue (see Mitchell, p.22).

The difference between these two views is, however, not as great as it may seem to be. The view that there are certain rules which any society must have is unlikely to come down to an enumeration of those rules in completely specific terms. Rules concerning the protection of life and property can take various forms. That there must be such rules does not tell us what in detail they must say. No one is likely to want to maintain of any quite specific rules in these fields that they are necessary for any society whatever; on the whole people are now well aware of the danger of mistaking their own ways of arranging things for rules of universal validity. The view that there are some rules which are necessary for any society can be made to seem plausible if those rules are expressed in a sufficiently general way. (It is not merely plausible, of course: it also happens to be true). The more generally they are expressed, however, the less room there is likely to be for real disagreement with the contrary view that a society needs rules but not any in particular. It would be implausible, to take a much discussed example, to maintain that absolutely any society whatever needs monogamy. This would be to reject evidence of the existence of societies which seem to have successfully maintained themselves on a basis of polygamy. If the rule is expressed in a more general form — that a society needs some (any) accepted system of marriage — it certainly gains plausibility, but at the expense of particularity; and the supporter of the view that society needs rules but not any particular rules has now much less to quarrel with. If the process of generalization is taken still further, to the extent that all that is being maintained is that a society needs some principles of cohabitation, he may well, in practice, find virtually nothing to quarrel with. The institution of monogamy is an illustration used by Devlin himself. (The issue here is discussed interestingly by Mitchell.) Hart does not regard the rule of monogamy as a rule which every society needs: but an example of a specific rule about the protection of life or property could equally well have been taken; that is, a rule designed to meet a kind of hazard to life or a kind of infringement of property rights which is peculiar to a particular society. Such a rule could be regarded as deriving from a much more general rule or principle, and the movement from the general to the particular here, or from the particular back to the general, is an easy one. General rules have to be interpreted in particular terms, and most particular social rules can probably be subsumed under a not too large number of general social rules. We need both general rules and particular rules; and there would be something strained about regarding them as in some sense rivals. Every society needs rules, certainly; and every society, as Hart argues, needs some rules of a certain kind. The view that says that any rules will do may seem plausible when one thinks of some of the differences that undoubtedly exist between societies: societies seem to be able to hold together on rather various bases. At the same time, if it is indeed the case, as I have suggested, that widely varied and numerous particular rules of different societies can probably be subsumed under a limited number of general rules, there may well not be all that much difference between Hart's view on this point and that which is opposed to it.

We have noted that the philosopher is interested in three main kinds of social rule — moral, legal, and political. Let us now take up the question of relations between rules of these three kinds. Often rules can be distinguished in respect of their content, but sometimes this is not the case. Rules restricting the parking of motor vehicles are legal rather than moral or political; rules about the duties of respect owed by children to their parents are moral rather than legal or political; rules about the powers of the Prime Minister are political rather than legal or moral. On the other hand, rules against the taking of life are both legal and moral; and rules involving the notions of promise and contract are sometimes a mixture of all three elements. Because it is not possible to draw satisfactory distinctions between these three kinds of social rule with reference to their content alone it is necessary to look as well for differences between them of a formal kind.

Moral rules seem to be *more important* than other rules. We test legal and political rules by moral tests, and if they are found morally wanting this is taken to be a fault in them. We are less inclined to test moral rules by legal or political tests. If we adhere to a rule as a moral rule we will not consider that its failure to conform to some legal or political standard is a reason why we ought to give up our adherence to it. We may in fact cease to adhere to it; legal and political pressures can be very strong: but in doing so we are unlikely to consider that we are giving it up because we ought to give it up, but rather that we have been forced into giving it up. Indeed, it is probably a truism to say that we cannot suppose we *ought* to give up some rule which we regard as a *moral* rule: adhering to a rule on the ground that it is a moral rule involves believing that it is a rule we ought to follow. At the same time, some people do seem to invest legal and political rules with the sort of importance that most of us reserve for moral rules. Are we to say simply that, for them, what other people call legal and political rules are 'really' moral rules? This surely would be too easy a way of saving the point. It would make pointless the statement that moral rules are more important than other rules. It would be like saying, as is sometimes said, that there are 'really' no atheists, for whatever a man regards as being of ultimate concern is his God. If the consequence of this is that a man's stamp collection may qualify as his God then indeed there are no atheists, but there is also little point in calling anyone a theist. If moral rules are any rules that any man happens to regard as rules of overriding importance then the point of treating importance as a distinguishing mark of moral rules largely vanishes. It seems then that importance as a formal criterion of a moral rule cannot stand on its own feet. We need to take it in conjunction with other criteria yet to be mentioned.

A second point concerning the relation between moral, legal and political rules is the following. Breaches of legal rules are punishable by fines, or imprisonment, or the like. Breaches of moral, and to a lesser extent political, rules are 'punishable', in general, by little more than expressions of displeasure. In the case of breaches of political rules the displeasure may be accompanied by practical consequences — to the extent of the fall of a government — but it would be odd to use the term 'punishment' of these consequences. In the case of breaches of moral rules punishment may well take place, but it is in the form of social displeasure (which admittedly may go to the extreme of ostracism); fines or imprisonment would seem quite inappropriate, unless, of course, the rule in question had the double character of being both legal and moral. Different sanctions, then, are attached to legal and to moral and political rules.

Further, legal rules, and to some extent political rules, are formalized, as moral rules in general are not. True, there are moral codes, like the decalogue, whose rules are tabulated in as formal a way as are the political principles of a written constitution or the provisions of a law on the statute book. And some philosophers, such as Kant, have attempted to reduce moral rules to explicit formulations. However, there is a difference in this matter between moral rules and legal and political rules. Neither Kant's moral philosophy nor the decalogue (though in the latter case the situation is sometimes represented otherwise) *creates* moral rules. The formalization of the rules is a device to explain, or to recommend, moral principles, not to bring them into existence. Legal rules, however, can be created. When a bill is put upon the statute book a law is *created,* and this is a formal process. Some laws grow up, some are made. Moral rules always grow up; no one makes them. Moral rules are often said to be man-made, but the sense in which they are man-made is not that someone in particular makes them, in the way someone in particular can sometimes make laws. If they are man-made they are made by men in general, in a way that is not clearly formalizable and certainly not clearly datable (see Hart (2), p.171).

Moral rules are applicable to all mankind, in a way that other rules need not be. If I maintain that something is a moral rule I am maintaining that it is a rule for everyone, or at any rate for everyone in the same situation. If I hold that slavery is morally wrong this means that I believe it always to have been wrong. There is, of course, a sense in which morality is relative: societies differ in the moral rules to which they adhere. The Greeks, in general, approved of slavery and we, in general, do not. This is a difference between their moral attitudes and ours. But when someone today condemns slavery on moral grounds, part of what he means is that the Greeks were mistaken when they supposed slavery to be right. Equally, if an ancient Athenian or a nineteenth century slave owner said that he approved of slavery on moral grounds part of what he would mean would be that anyone at that time or subsequently who condemned slavery would be mistaken. Of course, the issue is not as simple as this. Approval or disapproval of slavery can be not on moral grounds but on the grounds of expediency; and it can be a qualified approval or disapproval. Nevertheless, despite the undoubted relativity of morality, for a rule to be a moral rule it must be *claimed* to be of universal applicability. If someone said, 'The ancient Greeks approved of slavery, we disapprove of it: we simply differ from them in that respect', we should hardly say that any *moral* rule was implied in what he was saying. If he said, 'Slavery is wrong and in approving of it the Greeks were mistaken' we should be willing to say that a moral rule was involved. In general we do not make these claims to universal validity in the case of legal and political rules. (I do not intend to deny outright the possibility of unique moral judgments — in cases where someone may wish to claim that there are certain circumstances which in principle can never recur and in which a certain course of action is right. However, in such cases we are not dealing with moral *rules* so much as with what are claimed to be unique moral *judgments,* presumably not subsumable under any rules, and the question of the universal applicability of moral rules is therefore not affected, or at any rate not directly.)

It has sometimes been argued that another feature of moral, as opposed to legal and political, rules is that every man's moral rules must have been adopted by his own decision. Most of us adhere to moral principles that we have inherited from our parents and teachers. The view at present under consideration would regard us, if we go no further than this, as enjoying at best an undeveloped morality, at worst no morality at all. A man's morality must be something that he has consciously chosen for himself. This view, however, has the defect that it denies the name of morality to the only kind of morality that many people have. The conscious adoption of moral principles requires a degree of self-consciousness about moral principles that a great many people surely do not possess. They adhere to moral principles out of habit, not conscious decision. Nevertheless, it is easy to see what is meant by saying that there is something undeveloped about such a habitual morality. There is certainly a sense in which morality is something that a man makes his own. Men may also adhere in this deliberate way to some political principles, though they are less likely to behave thus in the case of legal rules.

The foregoing discussion has brought out some differences between moral, legal, and political rules. But at the same time it must be recognized that there are difficulties in finding completely clear-cut points of difference. From some points of view we find moral and political rules sharing a certain feature as against legal rules; from other points of view it may be political and legal rules which share a feature as against moral rules. It would, of course, be possible to achieve greater sharpness by legislating that nothing will be allowed to count as a moral rule unless it has such-and-such a formal feature. For example, we might adopt the criterion of deliberate adherence as our *sine qua non*. But such a procedure would obscure the interesting complexity of the relationship between moral, legal and political rules — a relationship which is in the end made up of a mixture of likenesses and differences. For our present purposes it is more valuable to recognize that there is a large class of what can usefully be called social rules rather than to seek too closely to differentiate between various members of this general class. Naturally, this position begs some questions. In particular, some might claim that it is misleading to describe moral rules as 'social' rules at all, for this suggests the wrong sort of status for them. But the description of them as social rules is not intended to close any doors against inquiry about the precise status of moral rules. Whatever else they are, they are *at least* social rules in the sense of rules governing the life of men in society. The question of the status of moral rules has exercised philosophers much more than that of the status of legal and political rules. Perhaps this reflects the recognition of the special importance which, as we have noted, has been commonly claimed as a feature of moral rules. But the fact that there are problems here ought not to prevent us from treating moral rules, on one level, as members of the large class of social rules.

A distinction is sometimes drawn between public and private morality, and a related distinction has been drawn between social and individual morality. The reason behind the drawing of such distinctions is the recognition of a particular kind of conflict within morality — or, as some might prefer to put it, between two moralities. Sometimes a man's conscience leads him to conclude that something ought to be done which conventional, 'public' morality either does not recognize as needing to be done or believes ought not to be done; that is, an individual's moral convictions may be in conflict with the moral beliefs and practices of his society. The conflict may take the fairly serious form of a conflict between 'individual value' and 'social value'; that is, a man may put his own welfare first and sincerely believe that he has good moral reasons for this, whereas 'society' puts the welfare of the community first: the belief that charity begins at home — a moral belief — may bring a man into conflict with a morality whose basis is wider. Does a society have the right to impose its moral standards upon its members; or, to reverse the question, does the individual have the right to act in accordance with private moral convictions against the beliefs and practices of the society in which he lives?

We have in the preceding paragraph not one but several questions. The issue as between 'public' and 'private' morality, or 'social' and 'individual' morality, is a many-sided one. The influence of individualism upon the thinking of people in our society is strong — as we noted in the first chapter. If put to the test, the average man in our society would be likely to say that in the long run a man ought to do what his own conscience tells him. But this answer is itself a conventional answer — the answer which the morality of our society has impressed upon us. This lends a certain air of unreality to the conflict. At other times and places, where an individualistic morality is less strongly developed, the very possibility of such a conflict is less. There public or social morality may seem the only morality there is. The idea that it might be right to do something for one's own good as opposed to the good of society — for example, to amass a large private fortune by exploiting the labour of the less fortunate (or less 'deserving'), though it would naturally not be put in quite those terms

— is unlikely to occur to people whose only morality is a public or social morality. It is when morality has come to be thought of as a matter primarily of personal relations and duty to one's immediate family and friends that the possibility of conflict between what is best for the individual moral agent and what is best for society becomes real. Paradoxically, as we have noted, the very developments in men's moral outlook which give rise to the possibility of conflict also contain its solution. We need to be aware that it is not a solution offered from an entirely neutral standpoint. It is a solution valid for our society, as the problem is a problem valid for our society. At the same time this is not meant to imply that the problem (and its solution in individualistic terms) is entirely culture-bound; both the problem and this solution of it may well have a broader foundation than that.

Morality is a mixture of the individualistic and the social. Which element is uppermost is a matter of history. Though the bias of our own society is more towards individualism than was that, say, of the ancient Greeks, doubtless most systems of morality contain elements of both. There is a connexion between the individualistic or the 'private' approach in morality and the tendency to see moral rules as regulations. A view which understands moral rules in terms of the model of regulations is not, of course, totally committed to seeing moral rules as imposed 'from outside'. It is the case that regulations typically are imposed from outside — by an authority — and it is true that some moral views do see moral rules as divine imperatives or as commands of Reason (where Reason is understood as something more than the reason of the individual himself on whom the rules are binding). But regulations can also be self-imposed: one can make rules for oneself, as opposed to having them imposed by outside authority, or one can by conscious decision adopt as one's own rules certain social conventions.

We need to exclude from the notion of regulations here the suggestion, which 'regulation' usually carries, of temporal and spatial limitation. Regulations are typically set up at a particular time and may be rescinded at another time; and they typically apply to particular stated classes of people. Moral rules, however, as we noted earlier, cannot be created by anyone's decision, and those who hold them would claim for them universal validity. So the sense in which moral rules can be held to be regulations is a qualified sense. Nevertheless, moral rules have often been seen as a kind of super-regulation ('the Moral Law'), imposed by a supreme authority and of universal validity. As we have just remarked, they have also at other times been seen as regulations that a man adopts for the conduct of his own life; regulations which he does not suppose to be God-given but which he equally does not suppose to be merely his own creation, for he would claim for them a universal validity as much as would the believer in their divine origin. To see moral rules in terms of the model of regulations is, then, not uncommon. Such views need to be distinguished from those that adopt the model of regularities. Here moral rules are seen as stating features of what people do as social creatures. The morality of one society is sometimes contrasted with that of another: such a contrast will be partly in terms of what people in each of the societies say and partly in terms of what they do. In such a contrast we are concerned less with what ought to be done than with how people in fact behave, which will include what they say about what ought to be done. The discussion in such cases is on the descriptive rather than the normative level.

It was perhaps natural for philosophers, who have themselves been much more self-conscious about moral rules than have non-philosophers, to suppose that it is necessary for everyone to be self-conscious about moral rules — to suppose that a rule cannot be a moral rule unless it is consciously adhered to or recognized as a binding rule imposed by some authority. The morality of non-philosophers, however, is less a matter of rules recognized or adopted by the individual and more a matter of social convention; though in our society, as we have noted, it does have a built-in individualistic bias which tends to come to the surface whenever for some reason moral rules have to be made explicit and be examined. It is natural for philosophers to think of moral rules as regulations (with qualifications) rather than regularities; but the view of moral rules which sees them mainly as social regularities is probably preferred by students of society who are not philosophers.

A word of warning is necessary. Social rules, including moral rules, need to be distinguished from social customs, which also are regularities of a kind; the description of social rules as the expressions of social regularities is not intended to suggest that there is no difference between the rules of a society and the customs of that society.

Social rules are perhaps a mixture of regulations and regularities, but in social rules some element of regulation (or rather, some normative element) must be present, however strongly the emphasis may be placed in a particular view on regularity rather than regulation. The distinction that is being used here between regulations and regularities is a distinction between two different kinds of rules, not one between rules and something other than rules. The term 'regularity' is ambiguous, as it might be taken as referring to behaviour of a purely 'mechanical' kind: this is not the sense intended here.

The philosopher studies social rules. His interest is, as always, in getting clear the meanings of concepts. He wants to find out what constitutes a social rule, and what is the relation of one kind of social rule to another. The philosopher is not interested in laying bare the particular set of social rules that obtain in any given society. He is interested in more general questions.

To know what a social rule is, is to have gone a long way towards knowing what life in society is, and therefore what human life is. It is from this beginning that it is possible to go on to the study of particular societies. The social anthropologist, in approaching the study of the society he has chosen for investigation, needs to do so with the concept of a social rule firmly fixed in his mind; though preferably without too firm a grasp upon the precise subdivisions of it with which he is familiar in his own society. That is to say, the Western social anthropologist ought not to look too determinedly for political rules, legal rules, moral rules, religious rules. The social rules of the society he is studying may not divide up so neatly. If they do divide up neatly perhaps they divide up into different classes. Perhaps the category of the political and that of the religious do not fall apart so sharply as he would expect them to with the example of his own society behind him. Yet the *concepts* of the political, the legal, the moral, the religious, are separable from each other (even though linked in various ways). These concepts, and others, he will need to make use of. What he needs to be careful about is expecting the facts to fit neatly into these categories. The categories are useful. The trouble comes, if it comes, through too unquestioning an acceptance of sharp differences between them and too unquestioning an application of them.

The philosopher, then, sets out to offer some account of a social rule, and related concepts. Given the fact of societies, given the fact of such-and-such social behaviour, one thing we can conclude is that there must be social rules. It is a condition of the existence of societies that there should be what we call social rules. To recognize the concept of a social rule, and to study the nature of social rules, their varieties, their interconnexions, and the question how far certain rules may be necessary, are not the least important of the things that philosophers do.

# CHAPTER 4

# Utilitarianism

PHILOSOPHERS have taken a deeper interest in moral than in legal or political rules: partly, no doubt, as we have suggested, because they have recognized their greater 'importance', and partly because morality lends itself more easily than does politics, or even perhaps law, to expression in individualistic terms and therefore accords well with philosophical interests since the seventeenth century. At any rate, a good deal of philosophical energy has been expended on the development of theories of morals and the defence of each against its rivals. Philosophers have tried to reduce morality to its first principles. They have tried to produce general theories of ethics that impose some clear, simple pattern upon moral thinking and practice.

Of such theories Utilitarianism has a particular interest for the student of society in that it is the philosophy underlying the Welfare State. The name Utilitarianism usually means Pleasure Utilitarianism or Hedonistic Utilitarianism, the doctrine that pleasure or happiness is the ultimately good thing and that the criterion of the rightness of actions is conduciveness to human happiness. That Utilitarianism is associated with reform, or social improvement — both Jeremy Bentham and J. S. Mill were notable reformers — is an indication at least that its heart is in the right place; though this has not secured for it immunity from criticism.

An objection is commonly urged against the identification of the ultimate moral end with pleasure or happiness. Some maintain that the development of character, through self-discipline or self-sacrifice, is more important than happiness. Mill himself, as it happens, laid a good deal of stress on the building of character; but not enough stress, it seems, to please the critics. And although he also considered that

Utilitarianism did acknowledge the importance of self-sacrifice, he insisted (and the critics deny) that there is no virtue in self-sacrifice for its own sake but only for the sake of the general happiness. There are other moral points of view than that of Utilitarianism. To someone who believes that, say, conscientiousness for its own sake has great moral value, pleasure or happiness as an end of life may not seem to rank very high. Mill supposed that considerations could be brought forward to show that happiness is indeed the ultimate desirable thing. He fully recognized, however, that no real proof could be found of any view about ultimate ends. That conscientiousness is the ultimate end is thus, from his point of view, as incapable of real proof as is the view that happiness is. Rival views to Utilitarianism do exist — views which are apparently neither absurd nor without support of the kind that Mill supposed could be found for the Utilitarian doctrine, namely, that men of experience can be found who do in fact believe that something other than happiness is of ultimate value.

Utilitarianism may seem to possess at least the virtue of great simplicity. It might be claimed for it that it offers a simple solution in situations of moral conflict: it is necessary only to discover which of two proposed courses of action conduces more to the general happiness. But, say the critics, too much simplicity is not necessarily a virtue in a moral theory. How are degrees of happiness to be measured and compared? Suppose there are differences between the qualities of happiness involved and not merely differences of quantity? Mill supposed that there were higher and lower kinds of pleasure, and on this supposition there might well be difficulties in deciding whether or not a smallish amount of a noble pleasure should be preferred to a rather large amount of a less noble pleasure. Utilitarianism is also held to be over-simple in its concentration on consequences: in assigning moral worth to an action we do not in fact limit ourselves to its consequences, possible or actual, but also take account where necessary of the motive from which it is done or of the character of the action itself (as being an action, say, of promise-keeping or of truth-telling). Act-Utilitarianism (the doctrine that individual actions must satisfy the criterion of conduciveness to human happiness) is a more simple view than Rule-Utilitarianism (the doctrine that it is classes or kinds of action — e.g., actions of promise-keeping in general — that must satisfy the criterion and that individual actions are right if they fall under a rule enjoining such a kind of action). Mill himself may have been a Rule-Utilitarian. He also allowed some place to motives, though he claimed that these have to do with the moral worth of agents rather than of actions. Certainly Mill's version of Utilitarianism possesses enough complexities to make the charge that Utilitarianism is an over-simple theory hard to establish. It is a charge more fairly made against the Utilitarian theory of Bentham. Mill may well be considered to have gone some way to meet criticism; and Henry Sidgwick went even further. Utilitarianism is capable of development. It is a fault in dis-cussion of moral theories that it often tends to involve the setting-up of Aunt Sallies; what is discussed is a generalized doctrine rather than the view of any particular writer. (Admittedly, this is a trap that it is practically impossible to avoid falling into.) The works of Mill, and even more of Sidgwick, undoubtedly offer more subtle views than what is often represented as Utilitarianism.

Another common objection is that the principle of utility may come into conflict with that of justice. Mere increase of total happi-ness is not of itself good; there is the further question of how this happiness is distributed. Might we not judge preferable a state of affairs in which fewer people were happy but those the most deserv-ing, than one in which more were happy but those the most vicious and undeserving? Mill did not believe that there can be any real con-flict between utility and justice, but Sidgwick was later to place a principle of Justice alongside that of Utility as a necessary comple-ment to it. Another form of the same objection is that if the general happiness is the only end, any means whatever to this end may seem to be justified — like punishing the innocent, if it leads to happiness on the whole. This point about punishment is generally countered by Utilitarians thus: the deterrent effect of punishing the innocent would almost certainly be less than that of punishing the guilty only, so that even on Utilitarian grounds it would not in fact be right to punish the innocent. However, this does not remove the real source of worry. If the Utilitarian refrains from punishing the innocent for this reason it is only a fortunate accident. He refrains from punishing the innocent because he sees that the utility of punishing the innocent is less than that of punishing the guilty. One may still be left with the impression that if the utility of it had been greater he would have been content to punish the innocent. No doubt it is this kind of consideration that leads people sometimes to contrast 'moral' with 'utilitarian' considerations, as if Utilitarianism were not a *moral* theory at all. There is no doubt that Utilitarianism, although it has been the inspiration of so much social reform, is in some versions open to the objection that it does not sufficiently take account of the worth of individuals. In some aspects, despite the individualistic elements in the thought of Bentham and Mill themselves, it runs counter to the individualistic emphasis characteristic of the moral theorizing of the past three centuries. The trouble no doubt springs from the interest of Utilitarians in ends. The step to the end justifying the means is easily taken. Then the fatal last step, to the end justifying any means, seems naturally to follow. However, the fact that Sidgwick refused to take it shows that it is not so much Utilitarianism that is at fault as a narrowly defined, rigid sort of Utilitarianism. As far as flexibility in the doctrine is concerned, Mill is an advance on Bentham, and Sidgwick on Mill.

It has also been made a charge against Utilitarianism that it commits the Naturalistic Fallacy — the fallacy, or alleged fallacy, of defining moral notions in terms of non-moral notions. There is however a version of Utilitarianism that avoids this. The theory known as Ideal Utilitarianism replaces 'happiness' by 'good': the criterion of rightness is seen as conduciveness to the greatest good. G. E. Moore, who mounted the attack on Mill as committing the Naturalistic Fallacy, was himself an Ideal Utilitarian. As we have noted, the pursuit of pleasure or happiness — even if it is no selfish pleasure but the greatest pleasure of the greatest number — is apt to strike some as a doubtful end for morality. At the same time, the virtues of Hedonistic Utilitarianism — in particular its recognition of the importance of consequences and its reformist atmosphere — may well seem worth preserving. Ideal Utilitarianism thus presents itself as an improved version of Utilitarianism.

The pursuit of pleasure has often been contrasted with the moral life; so that however one refines the notion of pleasure there is likely to be some suspicion of a theory which seems actually to identify the moral life with the pursuit of pleasure. Even if we read 'happiness' for 'pleasure' the suspicion is likely to remain: 'the pursuit of happiness' still has a ring to it which some might want to contrast with 'the truly moral life'. Of course, such suspicions may be quite unfounded;

but Mill recognized their force and felt that to persuade men to accept Utilitarianism — that is, Hedonistic Utilitarianism — required an effort of argument. It may be that there is sometimes also an element of selfishness concealed within the notion of the maximization of pleasure or happiness. At any rate, the charge of selfishness has been brought against Utilitarianism. It is not, I think, a fair charge; but it finds support in the fact that Bentham attempted to combine Utilitarianism with Psychological Egoism (the doctrine that we are so constituted as to be unable to seek anything but our own pleasure), and by the further fact that even Mill, in one passage in his *Utilitarianism,* writes as though the pursuit of individual happiness could somehow be transmuted into a general pursuit of the general happiness. In making his attempt Bentham was being illogical, and in feeling bound to support him Mill showed more loyalty than logic. At any rate, however well- or ill-founded are its critics' suspicions of selfishness, Utilitarianism has had to suffer them. By abandoning the notions of pursuit of pleasure or of happiness and replacing them by that of pursuit of good, Ideal Utilitarianism allays the suspicions. No one would be likely to understand the pursuit of good as including an element of selfishness.

Nevertheless, Ideal Utilitarianism has its faults too. Suppose we find ourselves in a situation where we could do more good by breaking a promise or by telling a lie than by keeping the promise or by telling the truth. We should probably not think it right to break the promise or to tell the lie. Suppose an old friend on his deathbed, with no other witnesses present, asks me to promise that when he is dead I will visit on his behalf a film star whose devoted fan he has been for years. I promise. Should I keep this promise or not? If I do, in all probability the film star will not receive me; she is notorious for her lack of interest in her followers. It will cost me money which I could put to better use — say, by contributing the fare to a charity. The dead man is no longer in a position to care. If the moral end is the maximization of good then surely it will be my duty not to keep my promise but to find a better use for the money it would cost me to do so. Yet this goes against our ordinary moral convictions. I have promised, and promised in particularly solemn circumstances. My duty surely is to carry out my promise. It would be immoral for me to do anything other than what I have promised to do — or so it is claimed. The critics of Ideal Utilitarianism maintain, then, that there are certain moral questions to which the Ideal Utilitarian is forced by his theory to give what is clearly the wrong answer, and that this demonstrates the inadequacy of the theory.

Now it is true that the thought of breaking a solemn promise makes most responsible people feel uncomfortable. But it is at least possible that this is because they have not examined their own moral notions closely enough. It is undoubtedly the case that we do tend to think that promises are sacred — especially, no doubt, promises made to people on their deathbeds — but why do we tend to think this, and do we think it in absolutely all cases? There may be an element here of belief in an unseen heavenly Witness of all that we do, who will know that we have broken our promise and will somehow see that we are punished for it. If this seems too naïve we perhaps need reminding that notions like that of the sacredness of promises, which we learn in our very earliest days, may well come to us originally accompanied by such associations, and although we may suppose that these associations play no part whatever in our present convictions it is not an easy matter to determine how much our feeling that all promises are sacred may nevertheless still owe to them. Many of our moral convictions are normally unexamined, and things are apt to seem self-evident simply because they are never challenged; but to be unchallenged is not to be unchallengeable. In any case, the proposition that promises are sacred is one to which most of us would in fact admit exceptions. Suppose, to go back to the earlier example, I had promised my friend on his deathbed that I would do something bad. If I afterwards repented and broke my promise would this be so offensive to the ordinary moral consciousness? Suppose he hated his employer and had long wanted to shout abuse at him, but had been afraid to do so in case he laid himself open to dismissal or to legal proceedings. Suppose he had prepared a letter to his employer so that he would have the satisfaction of knowing as he died that he was going to convey his opinion of him at last without any fear of reprisals. The promise he asks me to make (again, without witnesses) is that I will post this letter for him after he is dead. I promise, and promise in complete sincerity. Afterwards, however, I think better of it on the grounds that to send the letter will do no good to anyone living but will in fact cause harm. I should have argued in accordance with the principles of Ideal Utilitarianism.  In this case it is surely likely that my argument in defence of breaking a promise would be approved by the ordinary moral consciousness.  Promises are not always sacred; the exceptions are cases where what is promised is something bad.  The critic is right to point out that Ideal Utilitarianism cannot account for cases where we think it right to do something because we have promised, even though we believe that the doing of it may decrease the total amount of good in the world.  But there are also cases where, by contrast, we do argue in an Ideal Utilitarian way and break promises for the reason that to keep them would decrease the total amount of good in the world.

That men have a certain conviction, a conviction that promises ought to be kept irrespective of whether the keeping of them tends to an increase of good in the world, is not the end of argument but rather the beginning.  We need to inquire in what circumstances this conviction operates and in what circumstances it does not; for a little reflection will show that it is not true to say that most people believe that it is *invariably* right to keep a promise when we could do more good by breaking it.  If the Ideal Utilitarian claims that the *only* moral consideration is the increase of good then his claim is not borne out by the ordinary moral consciousness.  Nevertheless, this is an extremely powerful moral consideration.  The point is not that Ideal Utilitarianism is a bad moral theory, but that it is a theory that does very well for some cases but not so well for others.  This indeed, is an all too common feature of moral theories.

It would be idle to deny that Utilitarianism — whether Hedonistic or Ideal — has faults.  So, however, have other moral theories.  It also has solid virtues.  There is no existing moral theory of which a critic cannot say that it is one-sided or over-simple; though naturally its supporters will argue that the one-sidedness or over-simplicity is imaginary, or, if real, justified.  It may be that there is a fundamental mistake at the heart of the very idea of producing a simple moral theory — that our moral thought and practice is so complex that no single theory ever could be found that would do justice to it.  The attempted reduction of complexity to simplicity seems to be a feature of moral theories, however, and it is unlikely that all philosophers will give up permanently all interest in searching for some relatively simple formula.  They will want to avoid what seems to them the wrong kind of simplicity; but some kind of simplicity they are likely to go on wanting. Utilitarianism has content, whereas some other philosophical approaches tend to limit themselves largely to explaining the formal properties of moral utterances. It offers arguments in support of itself which are not wholly without merit, whereas its traditional rival, Intuitionism, tells us that certain things are right, certain other things are wrong, but that we must not ask why they are right or wrong. Furthermore, Utilitarians think that social improvement is important. It remains true, nevertheless, that social improvement can take place without a general moral theory to back it up, and I am, of course, not suggesting that it is a sufficient reason for adopting Utilitarianism that it has a close association with social reform.

# CHAPTER 5

# Human Action and Free Will

IN this chapter I take up for closer examination some points that have been made in previous chapters — points centring round the notion of meaningful action.

Human actions are of many kinds, from the making of wills to the making of coffee, from the signing of treaties to the signing of autographs. There are, however, beneath this rich variety, some very general features that human actions have in common. They are not to be accounted for in purely causal terms, and they have a social context.

Consider the situation of a number of men pursuing each other and an oval ball about a field. A causal account, in physical or physiological terms, can be given of what is going on. The movements of the men's muscles, their occasional falling to the ground, their putting of their arms about one another in a spider formation — all this can be explained in causal terms. But what is it that is thus explained? Does such an account explain that they are playing rugby? How do we distinguish in causal language between practising playing rugby and actually playing it? Or between a move in the game that is successfully executed in accordance with a plan and one that is simply a stroke of luck? Between attacking and tackling? An account in terms of the bodily movements of the men on the field is not adequate to settle questions like these. One way in which we in fact settle them is by referring to the players' intentions and purposes and motives. Words like 'intention', 'purpose', 'motive', have no place in the vocabulary of causal explanation. Causal explanations will do as accounts of human behaviour and of what happens to people, but they will not do as accounts of human action. They do not allow us to make distinctions that we want to make — that, indeed, we are bound to make if the concept of human action is to be adequately distinguished from those of behaviour and happenings.

Again, we could not adequately explain what the men on the field were doing without reference to the social context in which their action is going on. To play rugby is to do certain things in accordance with a set of rules and conventions. The players on the field did not themselves invent those rules and conventions. They have a history and a present social context, and unless we take some account of that history and context we shall not understand what is going on. This is not to say that we must be consciously attending to such knowledge while we watch them, or even that we need ourselves actually possess this knowledge in detail. The point is a logical one, not psychological or biographical. An account of what the game of rugby is must involve reference to the rules and conventions of rugby; and the rules and conventions of rugby cannot in turn be defined in terms simply of a given game of rugby: its being a game of rugby at all is dependent upon its conformity with these rules and conventions, which therefore have an existence independent of their exemplification in it. When in 1823 William Webb Ellis picked up the ball and ran with it, he is sometimes said to have 'invented' the game of rugby football; but if this has any meaning at all it is a meaning conferred by hindsight. What he actually did on that occasion was to break the rules of the game he was supposed to be playing. The conventions and rules of games change, or are changed, from time to time; but what changes or is changed must already exist in order to change. We cannot, then, understand what someone who is engaged in playing a game is doing simply in terms of the movements or stratagems that he is going through or employing on that occasion.

This is true not merely of the action of playing a game. All actions fall into kinds. To understand what kind of action someone is performing (for instance, whether the off-hand candidate in an interview is not trying hard enough to get the job or is trying hard not to get the job), it is insufficient to consider his performance simply as the set of auditory and other behaviours peculiar to that occasion. Understanding would seem to require comparison and classification. In this sense at least, every human action has, and must have, a social context. Not only does understanding an action require description. Even to be able to identify something as an action at all is impossible unless we are able to say what *kind* of action it is. There is no action that is not an action of such-and-such a kind. There can be no actions that are incapable of being described. If a man goes through certain motions (as in miming) and then says, 'I have just performed an action', we can ask him, 'What action?' It is true that he does not need to answer by *naming* his action; it may have no name. We will, however, expect him to be able to describe in words what he has done. 'I waved my right hand four times up and down while shuffling my left foot.' Here he is describing his action by naming its parts. Whatever is not in some way describable or classifiable is not yet an action. An 'indescribable action' is not an action. We can generally refer to the agent's intentions, or his purposes, or his motives, and to do any of these things is to give some kind of account of his actions. To identify his motives, intentions, purposes, is to classify his actions — as those of a jealous man, or a man repairing a television set, etc. In however many respects a man's situation may be unique, if we are to understand it at all we must be able somehow to connect it with the familiar. It is hardly necessary to say that intentions are not motives, and motives are not purposes; and that neither intentions nor motives can be further identified with 'the reason for', or 'the point of', actions (the reason for an action is sometimes a more specific thing than its motive). But what we need to note is that 'With what intention?' or 'With what purpose?', etc., is the *kind* of question we very often need to ask about actions: this does not mean that there are not other questions that it is also relevant sometimes to ask. There are actions performed apparently without a reason, pointless actions, actions done seemingly unintentionally, or with no purpose in view, or apparently not motivated. When Meursault, in Camus's *L'Étranger,* murdered the man on the beach, he acted; yet he could not provide a reason for what he had done. But we can go on asking for a reason.

The notion of *unconscious* motives may be thought to create a difficulty for the position I have been presenting, namely that actions are social in the sense that they are classifiable — classifiable, that is, in terms of people's motives, intentions, purposes, etc., normally with regard to each other. It is a commonplace that the motives from which people act are not always what they themselves suppose them to be. Perhaps some unconscious motives, because they are unknown, may be indescribable, unclassifiable, unique. And if so, there may be at least the possibility that the actions which they motivate are themselves unique. What are we to say to this suggestion?

The concept of unconscious motives is not always directly relevant to human action. What is called an unconscious motive may act as a *cause*. Then, however, we are in the sphere of behaviour rather than action. Freud himself may well have thought of the operation of the unconscious in largely causal terms. Some of the metaphors used by Freudians to expound their view of the mind tend to suggest a causal interpretation. The metaphor of the iceberg — of the mind as mostly 'submerged', with the conscious occupying only the small part that is above the surface — is a causal one; movements of the iceberg beneath the surface *cause* movements of the part that is above the surface. Similarly with the metaphor of censorship, with its tendency to summon up the image of an entity, the Censor, stationed at the 'door' of the unconscious, allowing only certain thoughts to come through into the conscious. On this interpretation it is difficult to see that the concept of unconscious motive has much to contribute to the discussion of human action. If we look at the matter in this way we may reasonably conclude that the dividing line between action and behaviour has been wrongly drawn: that much more than we supposed of what human beings do is to be described as behaviour rather than action. This would be the effect of putting the stress on the word 'unconscious' in the expression 'unconscious motive'. However, it is not certain that Freud's theories really have the effect of extending the causal interpretation of what people do. They might equally well be taken as suggesting that the line ought to be moved in the other direction (putting the stress now on 'motive' rather than 'unconscious' in the expression 'unconscious motive'): metaphors, after all, are metaphors, and not to be taken literally. What is certain is that Freud's ideas are intended to make some difference to how we understand the things that human beings do. The term 'unconscious motive' suggests both a penetration of the causal into the sphere occupied by intentions and purposes, and a reverse penetration of something like intentions and purposes into the sphere of the causal. It suggests a refusal to be contented with an unexamined positioning of the dividing line between human behaviour and human action.

The question posed above was: may not unconscious motives be indescribable, and therefore (in terms of the account given) may they not be unique? Freud himself seems not to have supposed them to be either of these things. The contents of the unconscious that he was chiefly interested in far from being unique are supposed to be common to all males. They are also certainly describable. Freud has described them. They are the urge to murder one's father and have sexual intercourse with one's mother. As for the other contents of the unconscious, these derive from our experiences, and there is no reason to suppose these experiences unique or indescribable. If unconscious motives are in fact not indescribable or unique, their alleged indescribability or uniqueness cannot be held to constitute a reason for the indescribability or uniqueness of actions of which they are motives.

So far we have been considering two senses in which human action may depend upon a social context, first, that in which it depends upon general rules and conventions socially established, and, secondly, that in which it depends upon what we have been calling (for short) classifiability. There is now another sense to be noted. The quality of an individual act is also dependent in a more specific way upon its social context. Let us return to the example of an interview. The actions of the man being interviewed may be greatly affected by the atmosphere in which he finds himself. If the questions are not searching and the interviewers seem uninterested in his answers he may fear that he is not regarded as a serious candidate. How he reacts to this situation will vary. Perhaps he will set himself to force them to pay attention to him. Perhaps he will abandon hope and cease to make any effort at all. On the other hand, the interviewers may be aggressive and he may fear that they are determined not to have him at any price. Again, how he then acts towards them (how he 'reacts') will vary. How we act in specific circumstances depends upon those circumstances. This is the reverse of the coin whose obverse we have so far been examining. Alongside the generality of dependence upon rules or conventions and upon classification or description we need to place the particularity of circumstances. Just as the existence of society and hence of social contexts is implied in there being actions at all, so specific social contexts go to determine the form taken by specific actions.

Action is called forth by specific circumstances. Very often those circumstances include the action, or the behaviour, of other people.

If it were not for other people's demands upon us we should *act* much less frequently than we do. If, like Oblomov, we withdraw from responsibility and decision, the opportunities for action open to us are naturally much reduced. If we were left alone, unstimulated by others — unprovoked by them to anger, or love, or despair, or puzzlement — we should probably *do* very little. It is because we are not alone, because we are not allowed to be alone, that actions of many kinds become necessary. We have to work to live and working involves the performance of actions. Our relations with the State require constant action — the filling-in of forms, compliance with this regulation and that. The mere existence of other people and of social and political institutions requires that we act, and the wide variety of ways in which other people act upon us determines the variety of our own actions.

It is, of course, not only towards other people that we act. We can act towards a cat; or towards a stone. Nevertheless, the specific social contexts of our actions seem particularly important to them. The character of our motives, purposes, or intentions, and consequently the character of our actions, can vary much more with reference to people than to things. If I act with the intention of swatting a fly, then although my tactics may have to be changed rapidly many times as the fly moves about, the basic intention is not likely to change. I may become, with continued failure, more and more determined to swat the fly; but this intensification is not a radical change in my intention. I may in the end abandon the intention altogether; but to abandon an intention is not to change it. In my relations with other people, however, the possibility of a radical change in my intentions regarding them, or my purposes for them, or the motives from which I act towards them, is much greater. The way they act towards me may, as we saw in the example of the interview, radically alter my own motives, purposes or intentions and thus my own actions. We may have to adjust our intentions with reference to other people for the reason that they change their intentions with reference to us.

We have now noted three senses in which social context is important for action. First, action depends upon rules and conventions, and rules and conventions are social in character. Secondly, actions are classifiable in terms of motive, etc., and this normally requires social reference. Thirdly, a more specific sense: a great many actions — indeed, all our most important actions — involve in some quite precise way a physical relation with other individuals, and are formed and altered as a result of these relations; if we were not social beings only comparatively few actions, and those very limited, would ever be required of us.

It should perhaps be made clear that not all actions are social in this third sense. Nothing in the foregoing is meant to rule out the possibility of solitary action. But such action must be fairly rare. To act in such a way that the actions of other persons are in no way relevant to fixing the character of the action is possible. In such circumstances, however, a man is likely to lack motivation. Why act at all, if no one is prompting action? An objector might say to this: Even if no person is prompting action some thing may be. Suppose a man alone, faced with some threat of nature, say an avalanche. He must do something. He runs, or he tries to take shelter. He has been prompted to action; but not prompted by another person. Hence it is not only other persons who prompt us to action. People who live close to nature, or who get their living by wrestling with nature, are prompted to action by nature. The problems they have to solve by action are problems set them by nature. It is also possible for a man to be alone in his relations with nature, whereas it is (by definition) impossible for him to be alone in his relations with other men. All this is true. However, it is also true that our modern world is one where the possibility of being alone with nature is notoriously much less than it used to be. The sphere of non-social action is becoming less and less for modern, urbanized man. In any case, even where a man is alone, facing nature, his actions are still socially dependent in the second of the senses distinguished. We can describe and classify what he does. The man trying to escape from the avalanche is not the first man who ever tried to escape from an avalanche.

Even though solitary action in some sense may take place, the description and the occasion of actions seem, in the case of the former always and in that of the latter usually, to involve some kind of social reference. Living in society and performing actions are features of being human; and the actions we perform are largely determined by the fact that we live in society and in a particular sort of society. Consider the actions of a man having breakfast. His choice of cereal, his decision to have tea rather than coffee, the way he uses knife, fork or spoon — all this is socially dependent in obvious ways. The life of human beings is lived in society. The understanding of action generally speaking requires reference to social contexts.

It might be objected that the senses of social context distinguished in this chapter do not really enable us to distinguish clearly enough between action and behaviour. Behaviour, like action, might be said in a sense to follow rules and conventions and to be classifiable or describable; also, behaviour is sometimes dependent upon specific actions (and behaviour) of other people. This, however, would be to miss the significance of the references to intention, purpose, and motive in the foregoing. Human behaviour no doubt could in a sense be said to be subject to rules. It is predictable, at any rate, and no doubt whatever is predictable, whatever happens in a regular way, may be said in a sense to follow rules. It is not the sense in which I have written earlier in the book about rule-governed behaviour or action. The notion of following a rule is ambiguous. If something happens 'as a rule' — that is, usually — then it might be said *in a sense* to follow a rule. For instance, if a man usually, when drunk, hits people, we can say that 'as a rule' he hits people when he is drunk. We need not be imputing any intention or purpose to him. His hitting someone is a piece of behaviour, caused by his having drunk too much, not a deliberate act on his part; yet his behaviour does in a sense 'follow a rule'. (It would, admittedly, be difficult to construct a parallel case for 'convention' rather than 'rule'.) The sense, however, in which actions follow rules is different from this. I have just contrasted 'behaviour' with 'deliberate act'. The word 'deliberate' here brings out the contrast. Not all acts would, in fact, be described as deliberate, as we noted earlier; but in principle they all could be. That is, 'deliberately' (and some other words like 'purposely', 'intentionally') is a word that makes sense when used in the context of a description of someone's action. It never makes sense when used of behaviour. The man at the breakfast table is unlikely to pick up his knife deliberately. He has done this so often, and in circumstances where there is no real alternative, that the associations of hesitation, deep thought, effort, and so on, of the word 'deliberately' seem quite out of place. Still, although he is unlikely to pick up his knife deliberately, he could do so. Perhaps his wife has expressed her opinion he has already eaten as much toast as is good for him. He may say nothing in reply but deliberately take his knife in his hand ready to butter another piece.  Or perhaps when he takes up the knife it is with the intention not of buttering toast at all but of slitting his wife's throat.  Then he may well take it up deliberately.  It would never make sense, though, to use 'deliberately' in the context of an account of behaviour as opposed to action, or of something which happens to a man as opposed to something which he does.  A man may slip on a banana skin and fall.  We do not in this case say that he deliberately slipped on the banana skin or that he deliberately fell.  There are, of course, cases where we might say this.  For instance, he might be a comedian and have engineered the thing in order to raise a laugh.  But such cases are clearly cases not of behaviour but of action.  If someone leaps out at me unexpectedly I start, but not deliberately or intentionally.  Of behaviour or happenings we may use words like 'involuntarily', 'automatically', 'by reflex': we do not use 'deliberately', 'intentionally', 'purposely'.  The rules and conventions that govern action are rules and conventions that we are or can be aware of: so far behaviour and action run a somewhat parallel course; for we also can be aware of causes of human behaviour.  More importantly, however, they are also rules and conventions that can be deliberately broken as well as obeyed: here the concepts of behaviour and action diverge.  Behaviour may 'follow a rule', in the sense that something may happen 'as a rule', that is, usually.  In the case of action, not only can actions themselves follow a rule, in this sense, but a man *in* acting may himself follow a rule.  The sense in which a man's actions are to be attributed to him is not the same as that in which his behaviour is to be attributed to him.  He is the field in which his behaviour takes place; but he originates his actions.

We noted earlier the distinction between explanation in terms of causes and explanation in terms of motives, intentions and purposes. It might be objected, however, that the notion of cause is wide enough to include motives, intentions and purposes.  'What caused Jones to behave so atrociously towards his parents?'—'Snobbery'.  My intention of avoiding a too-talkative neighbour may cause me to approach my house from the other direction.  A house-painter paints a house with the purpose of preventing deterioration of wood and metal: this may be said to be what causes him to paint it.  These examples are not equally persuasive.  It is easier to see that motives can be called causes than that intentions and purposes (particularly purposes) can.

E

The intention of avoiding my neighbour, or the purpose of inhibiting rot or rust, is not so easily reified as is the motive of snobbery or jealousy or ambition. Ambition we easily think of as a kind of force, driving a man on; and therefore we easily think of it as functioning like a metaphorical efficient cause. Intentions and purposes — at least of the kind mentioned in my examples — do not lend themselves so easily to this sort of interpretation. The intention of avoiding a neighbour, or the purpose of inhibiting rot or rust we hardly think of as *forces*. I think there is no doubt that motives do seem to be causes to the extent that they seem to fit the stereotyped pattern of an efficient cause — the billiard cue which causes the billiard ball to move by striking it, to take a stock philosophical example. There are, of course, other senses of 'cause'. In particular, there is its sense in 'final cause', where to call a purpose a cause, far from needing defence, would be to make an analytic statement. There is little serious problem about whether motives, intentions and purposes are causes if we are allowed to understand 'cause' in a sufficiently wide sense; the wider the sense of 'cause' the less serious the problem. However, there is little point in asking 'Are motives causes of action?' unless one means by this to ask whether motives are causes of action in something like the sense in which the impact of the cue on the billiard ball is the cause of the latter's movement across the table. The distinction between motives and causes is a distinction between motive and a particular kind of cause. This does not preclude one's saying that motives, intentions and purposes may be causes in quite different senses of 'cause'.

It seems to me clear that the distinction between motives and causes stands, certainly as far as the topic of the present chapter is concerned. Even if we say that motives are in some sense causes it remains true that it is appropriate for an account of action to include reference to motives, and inappropriate for an account of the behaviour of billiard balls to do so. We do not abolish the distinction between action and behaviour by maintaining that motives are causes. The most this can do is complicate the statement of the distinction: the difference between action and behaviour now becomes that between goings-on the statement of whose causes may include reference to motives, intentions and purposes, and goings-on the statement of whose causes cannot include such references. We can choose between saying: (1) that the difference between action and behaviour is a difference between goings-on that may need terms like 'motive', 'intention', 'purpose' to be used in their description, and goings-on that cannot be described in these terms but that are adequately described in causal terms; or (2) that the difference between action and behaviour is a difference between goings-on whose causes generally include motives, intentions, and purposes and goings-on whose causes never include them. It does not much matter which of these we choose. In any case, none of this implies that motives, etc., are *nothing but* causes, or that there is *no difference at all* between action and behaviour. Attempts to argue that motives are causes have little to contribute to the understanding of human action.

The question must now be asked: has the discussion in this chapter established the distinction between action and behaviour? The answer can only be: that depends.

This distinction is one that is written into our language. We may not commonly pay much attention to it, but it is there, and we could not talk about people as we do unless we made use of it. At the same time, it is not certain that we could not manage without it. What we could not do without it is say all the things we now want to say about people; or, perhaps, although we could in a sense still say them — that is, we could still utter the same words — we could not mean what we commonly mean. It is not necessary to argue the impossibility of someone's carrying out the policy of being a consistent behaviourist. It is enough to point out that what he could say about human beings would be extremely limited. To go back to an example used at the beginning of the chapter, he could not easily distinguish between the case where people are playing a rugby match and that where the same people are practising playing rugby. This is not to say that he could not make any distinction at all. There might well be observable differences in the behaviour of the people in the two cases. But then these observable differences would for him be part of what he meant by the distinction between playing rugby and practising playing rugby: what for us is evidence for a certain thing for him would be part of the constitution of that thing. For the behaviourist the meaning of a human action can never be the same as it is for the non-behaviourist. It follows that the behaviourist cannot be talking about the same things as the non-behaviourist. It is not the case that the behaviourist is giving a different account of the same thing: he is giving an account of a different thing.

Perhaps behaviourism is not impossible. It is, however, exceedingly limiting. (Recall the discussion of the noise-and-movement approach in Chapter 2.) The discussion of action in this chapter does not demonstrate the difference between action and behaviour; it assumes it. Nevertheless, it does, I hope, have the effect of underlining the necessity of the concept of action for any account of persons and of society. We can do without this concept only if we are content to accept an extremely impoverished view of human beings. The behaviourist's view of human beings does not admit of what makes them human beings. A common argument in favour of behaviourism has been that it is 'scientific'. To argue thus, however, is to take a narrow view of science. We need not suppose that the human and social sciences must conform exactly to the model of the natural sciences. Anyone who supposed that unless they do they cannot be called 'science' would show little respect either for science or for human beings.

In the remainder of the present chapter I discuss briefly the concept of free will. In recent years the long-continuing dispute between free will and determinism has given way increasingly to the discussion of human action and related concepts. This is partly, no doubt, a matter of changing fashion. Partly, and more significantly, it reflects a real development, which consists in the attempt to make a fresh start on an old problem, to the extent, indeed, of redefining the problem as well as bringing new considerations to bear upon the answering of it. It would not be true to say, of course, that the controversy between free will and determinism in its more traditional form is therefore no longer worth taking seriously. Equally, it would be wrong to suppose that the interest of philosophers in the concept of human action is only a recent thing. It is an oversimplification to say simply that the contrast between action and behaviour that we have been considering so far in this chapter is the contemporary version of the more traditional contrast between free will and determinism. This is nevertheless a useful way of looking at the matter.

The controversy between libertarians and determinists has frequently been presented as one about whether an explanation in causal terms alone is adequate to account for our choices. Some libertarians claim that in choosing – or at any rate on some occasions of choosing (particularly occasions of moral choice) — a man acts contra-causally (see Campbell). The determinist denies this and supposes that all acts of choice can be adequately explained in causal terms. The libertarian appeals to intuition, to our immediate consciousness of being free at the moment of making a choice. The determinist answers that this 'immediate consciousness' may be illusory: perhaps our thinking ourselves undetermined is itself determined. The libertarian, this time with greater plausibility, now takes his stand upon the necessity of free will for morality. As Kant put it, freedom is a 'postulate' of the practical reason (i.e. of the moral faculty): we can make no sense of morality — in particular of duty — unless we suppose that we have freedom of choice; a man cannot have a duty to do what he is not able to do, and being able to do includes being able to choose to do. The concepts of freedom and duty are closely bound up together, so that we could not speak meaningfully of duty, in the sense that we normally give it, while denying the ability of men to exercise some control over their decisions: the consistent determinist is committed to denying meaning — or at any rate its normal meaning — to the notion of duty. This, however, does not refute determinism. It does refute the inconsistent determinist, the man who wants to have his cake and eat it. A consistent determinist, however, who is prepared to deny meaning to duty, is not affected by this argument. (It is fair to add that not all philosophers would agree that there is an incompatibility between determinism and morality).

It might be suggested that the libertarian case is stronger than I have made it out to be: that what we have here is not just two different views about duty — one normal, the other eccentric — but the true and only view of duty, which is an inescapable concept for human life in society, opposed to another which by denying or distorting this concept shows itself to be totally misunderstanding human life in society. The determinist is likely simply to reject this point of view. It might therefore seem that the libertarian can be more hopeful of success if he examines the determinist on his own position and looks for weaknesses there.

There can be no doubt that there are weaknesses in traditional determinism. The determinist case rests in part upon the belief that every event has a cause, that people's decisions are events, and that therefore they have causes. But, supposing that every event has a cause, it does not follow that explanation in terms of cause is the only kind of explanation, and that some other account of people's decisions may not also be needed in order to explain them fully. (The libertarian, for his part, is on weak ground if he asserts, as we have noted that certain libertarians do, that some decisions are 'contra-causal'.) Further, that 'every event has a cause' is a dictum that can give rise to differences of interpretation. What used to be called 'causal laws' in the natural sciences tend now to be regarded as statistical generalizations; in the social sciences they have probably rarely been regarded as anything else.

One marked feature of scientific method is prediction: the scientist, on the basis of his 'laws' or hypotheses is able to predict, with such-and-such a degree of certainty, that a given thing will happen; and the determinist case is made to rest in part also upon the claim that human behaviour is predictable. Now it is true that human behaviour is predictable, and often with a high degree of probability — both the behaviour of people in the mass and that of individuals well known to us. But from the fact that something is predictable it does not follow that it is determined — unless 'determined' means no more than 'predictable'; and if it indeed means no more than that the libertarian has little to fear. A man may tend to make the same choice in the same circumstances: that we can soon learn to predict what he will do does not mean that he is not nevertheless freely choosing on these occasions. Choice does not have to be unpredictable in order to be free. It is no doubt true that if behaviour were determined it would be predictable; but it is bad logic to suppose that therefore if it is predictable it is determined.

What is the determinist maintaining? Partly, that human behaviour is predictable. So it is, very largely. But he must be maintaining more than this, otherwise its predictability could not be put forward by him as evidence that human behaviour is determined: if a thing is evidence it must be evidence for something other than itself. What more then is he maintaining? Presumably, that human action or choice is caused, that a 'scientific explanation' can be given of it. So it can. But here, as we have noted, we need to bear in mind that a scientific explanation tends to be concerned merely with regularities of happenings: we have given up the belief in forces in nature. That there are regularities in the field of human choices can hardly be denied: libertarians do not usually claim that every act of choice is a miracle. The determinist, then, we may suppose, must be maintaining that a causal, or 'scientific', explanation of human choices is the only kind of explanation possible. Now to accept this would mean totally altering our way of looking at human beings; and it would be extremely difficult, and probably impossible, to carry through with complete consistency. The price the determinist asks us to pay is the making of an extreme intellectual effort, and the reward he offers for this effort is an inflexible and impoverished view of human beings. Of course, the reward the determinist thinks he is offering is greater than that. He might claim to be offering a 'scientific' view of man. But his view has been left as far behind by science as it is by a full all-round view of man.

To return to the subject of the earlier part of the chapter. There are alternative explanations of human behaviour/action — in terms of 'causal laws', environmental influences, etc., or in terms of intentions, purposes, motives, etc. The former can be given for all human behaviour/action; the latter only for that part of the complex of behaviour/action that is properly called action. Neither excludes the other. The reason for insisting on the latter as well as the former is the wish to preserve the dignity of humanity, the difference between persons and things and between persons and animals. The answer to the 'problem of free will' does not really lie in taking the side of libertarianism against determinism, or vice versa. Nor does it lie in attempts to show that there is no problem at all, because of linguistic or other confusions. It lies in a recognition, with Kant, that free will is bound up with the concept of a person. This is not proof, though Kant himself saw it as a kind of proof. It depends on the belief that persons are not things, and anyone is free to deny that belief. But anyone who accepts it is committed among other things to the concept of free will. Attempts to settle or prove anything in this field by independent argument are notoriously lacking in finality. An invitation to note the implications of one's everyday assumptions is all that can be offered, at any rate within the limits of this chapter, or, indeed, this book.

# CHAPTER 6

# Responsibility

IN the previous chapter we considered the concept of action — among other things, the difference between action and behaviour. This is a matter of practical as well as theoretical interest. Society may sometimes want either to encourage or to discourage certain kinds of action. Society may also sometimes want to encourage or to discourage certain kinds of behaviour. The methods appropriate to bringing about changes in people's behaviour are not always those appropriate to bringing about changes in people's actions. If we want to alter the actions of men we need to get them to alter their choices; whereas we may alter their behaviour by, for instance, working upon their emotions. No doubt by working upon men's emotions we can alter their actions as well as their behaviour; for by such means we can perhaps ultimately bring about in them new intentions and purposes. But whatever it is that brings about in a man new intentions and purposes, and whatever it is that leads him to make one choice rather than another, intentions, purposes, and choices must still be present (at least in principle) if what he does is to qualify as action at all. The category of action, as well as that of behaviour, is needed in any account of what men do; and this is recognized in any society or political system in which men are regarded otherwise than as merely something to be manipulated. Rational appeal, aimed at persuading men, by giving them good reasons, to adopt certain ways of doing things, is a method we are bound to use if we take human beings seriously. Whether or not it is an effective method is of less importance than the fact that we owe it to our fellow-men to use it. Naturally, it is not equally suitable to all circumstances: some subject matters are not easily argued about with non-experts. Further, it is possible to abuse it: some appeals to reason are undertaken in a patronising spirit. These, however, are hardly faults. There are various ways of showing respect for one's fellow men: this is one of them; and its natural implications are altogether opposed to the belief that human beings are simply things, whose behaviour can and should be made to conform to some end laid down for them by others.

Respect for persons includes treating them as rational. Part of what is involved in being rational is being responsible for one's actions. Responsibility is in turn closely linked with punishment. We do not consider a man deserving of punishment unless we think he was responsible for what he did. In the present chapter we shall discuss the concept of responsibility and in the following chapter that of punishment.

When is a man responsible for his actions? This is a question that used to be answered with a fair degree of confidence. 'A man is responsible for his actions when he does them of his own free will and not under duress.' However, both question and answer raise difficulties. They seem to imply that responsibility can be defined in terms of one or two positive properties possessed by actions, or by people. But this is at best too simple: we shall see that there are not one or two but many reasons why a man may be held responsible. At worst, it is seriously misleading: we shall see that responsibility is best explained not as a positive property or properties so much as (putting it roughly) an absence of properties. This is not to say that what we call the 'positive property' approach to responsibility has nothing whatever of value to contribute. A simple approach seems more immediately clear than a more adequate but more complex one: and not everything needs to be unlearned when a better method replaces a worse.

There is a useful distinction between 'responsible' used to assign people to a basic character category (responsible and irresponsible types) and 'responsible' used with reference to particular acts. 'No children under twelve years of age admitted unless in the company of a responsible adult' exemplifies the first of these senses, as does the talk about 'today's irresponsible youth' which has no doubt recurred in every generation. A responsible person is one who keeps appointments, does not default on hire-purchase payments, returns what he borrows, spends some of his money on food for his wife and children rather than all of it on beer and cigarettes for himself, and so on. An irresponsible person is one who possesses the opposite qualities. It is not difficult to fill out the meaning of 'responsible' and 'irresponsible' for our own society. Whether other societies would fill out the meanings of these words in the same way is another matter; but some sort of distinction between what we call responsible and irresponsible types is probably always necessary. Reliability and trustworthiness of some kind would seem to be part of the foundation of social organization. All this is to use 'responsible' and 'irresponsible' as labels for basic character types. This use is, as we noted, to be distinguished from its use when it refers to particular acts; that is, to someone's being responsible *for* some act – its use in the question with which the previous paragraph began. A man may be of the type we call irresponsible, yet he can be held responsible for his acts just as can a man of the type we call responsible. Commonly, part of what is involved in calling a man responsible for a certain act is that we think he is properly to be blamed for committing that act; there is a certain element of moral disapproval, or legal liability. As irresponsible people tend to draw upon them more in the way of blame than do responsible people, one might even suggest, paradoxically and not very seriously, that irresponsible people are more responsible than responsible people: this would be, of course, to trade on the ambiguity residing in the double sense of 'responsible'. On the other hand, some would say that irresponsible people are (probably for that reason) *not* to be held responsible for as many of the things they do as are responsible people. It is sufficiently obvious from these remarks that the two senses of 'responsible' are not unconnected. Indeed, this is only to be expected. What is not so clear is the precise nature of the connexion. At any rate, we are more concerned here with the distinction between the two senses than their connexion.

Philosophers have been mainly concerned with the second of the two senses of 'responsibility' – that where a man is said to be responsible for particular actions. In the present chapter it is this sense that we shall be discussing.

The traditional positive property answer leaves out something of considerable importance. Responsibility is, among other things, something that we *ascribe* to people (or that they ascribe to themselves). We *hold* people responsible. This aspect of responsibility is missed by the view which describes responsibility simply as some positive property or group of properties possessed by people themselves or by their actions. A man may possess the property of being red-haired or loud-voiced. It would not be natural to say we *ascribe* red-hairedness or loud-voicedness to him; and we do not *hold* him to be red-haired or loud-voiced. To call a man responsible for something is, in a way, to do something to him, and not merely to report on the presence or absence of some property or properties.

It may be that the inadequacy of the traditional view rests upon a failure to distinguish clearly enough between the two senses of responsibility that we have noted. In the first of these, to call a man responsible is to describe him — just as to call him red-haired or loud-voiced is to describe him. To call a man responsible, in this sense, is to say that he is reliable, honest, punctual, respectable-looking and so forth; and these words can all without difficulty be regarded as naming properties possessed by some people. We cannot easily give a precisely similar account of the second sense of 'responsible'. When we say that a man is responsible for some act we make a judgment about him in which we *ascribe* responsibility to him (or at any rate this is so in cases where we are *calling* a man responsible as opposed, say, to merely supposing him responsible — see Geach).

It is important to be clear about what it is to *ascribe* responsibility to people, or to *hold* them responsible. This must be distinguished from the social dependence of responsibility. What it means for a man to be responsible (first sense) will vary to some extent from society to society; and we might want to say that in a given society certain traits are *held* to constitute the sort of character that is called 'responsible' or the equivalent. It needs also to be distinguished from something else. Some people *hold* that the earth is flat; most of us *hold* that it is round; and, in general, whenever people are in dispute about something, it is natural to say that one side *holds* such-and-such while the other *holds* the contrary: if something is an undisputed fact it would be less natural to say that people *hold* it to be a fact. Now, in these cases, the holding is logically independent of what is held. Whatever it is that is held, its being held in no way goes to constitute its nature. It 'happens to be' held; but its nature would not be altered if it happened not to be held. What may be in dispute is clearly logically independent of the fact that one side in the dispute *holds* it and the other side does not *hold* it or holds its contrary. If what was in dispute was somehow logically dependent on its being held by someone or other, then there could never in fact be a dispute about it between parties one of whom held it and the other did not; for in such a case the parties logically could not be disputing about the same thing.

The kind of 'holding' that is involved in responsibility (second sense) is not of this logically independent kind. It is a necessary, though not a sufficient, condition for a man's being responsible for an action that he should be held (or should hold himself) responsible for it. An account of responsibility purely in ascriptive terms would be as one-sided as one in purely descriptive terms, that is, in terms of some property or properties supposed to be possessed by people or by their actions; but nevertheless, the ascriptive element cannot be ignored; and it is a fault of the traditional 'positive property' view that it largely ignores it. Naturally, a man is not *made* responsible for an action simply by having responsibility ascribed to him. Responsibility can be ascribed ignorantly or maliciously. There must be some reason for ascribing responsibility, some grounds for the ascription. There must be something about the person or about his act which justifies us in ascribing responsibility to him. To say this is to say something that may look very like what is said by the positive property view, namely, that a man is responsible for an action when he has performed it of his own free will and not under duress. We are not, however, bound to accept the traditional view as providing the only answer to the question of what features must be present before we can properly ascribe responsibility. The traditional view is both too positive and too simple. There are many features of an act and its agent that will be relevant to a judgment about responsibility.

It is necessary, however, to note that there is one sense in which a man's being responsible is in no way dependent upon his being held responsible. This is the causal sense of 'responsible', not in question here, where 'I am responsible for $X$' means simply 'I did $X$'. The word is seldom, in fact, used to say only this. We should not normally use it unless some question of praise or blame (usually blame) were involved. Normally, for a man to be responsible for something is for him not merely to have done it — though this also is a necessary condition of individual responsibility — but to be judged deserving of praise or blame for it. If we simply want to know who has done something, and we are not regarding it as a matter where praise or blame is involved, we should most naturally ask, 'Who did that?' To ask instead, 'Who is responsible for that?', would probably be taken as calling for the *culprit* to reveal himself. The fact that we more commonly have blame than praise in mind when we assign responsibility perhaps tells us something about men's attitudes to each other. However, there are some cases where we intend praise. If someone prepares the way for someone else's achievement we might say 'Jones did it but Brown was really responsible'.

The notions of shared responsibility, degrees of responsibility, direct and indirect responsibility, individual and collective responsibility, have given rise to a certain amount of controversy. Collective responsibility, in particular, has sometimes been considered morally offensive. It has been seen as a kind of shrugging off of responsibility from where it properly rests, namely, on the shoulders of individuals. 'It is not the accused who should be standing in the dock; it is society. Society has made him what he is.' 'No individual German was responsible for the rise and continued toleration of the Nazis; the whole German nation is responsible.' It is true that people sometimes try unfairly to evade their responsibility for something, or their share of responsibility, by assigning it to an abstraction, like society or the nation — or even mankind or human nature, as in the case of some religious doctrines about original sin. But the notion of collective responsibility has its acceptable uses, and is not to be dismissed as always only a device for unloading responsibility from where it 'properly' belongs. It is debatable whether responsibility must always 'properly' come home to the doors of individuals. There is often something of value in saying that society and not the criminal alone is responsible for the crime, that the apathy or greed of a nation is responsible for disastrous political developments. Although there are obvious difficulties involved in laying responsibility at the door of a collectivity or an abstraction it would sometimes be unfair to insist on assigning it solely to individuals. It can sometimes be just as morally offensive to insist on locating sole responsibility with an individual as to insist on locating it in an abstraction or a group.

We have already noted that the causal sense of responsibility — '*A* is responsible for *X*' means '*A* did *X* — has little to do with the topic we are discussing, apart from providing a necessary condition for the kind of responsibility that we are mostly interested in. It may be, however, that this causal sense of 'responsibility' makes some subliminal contribution to the insistence sometimes encountered upon individual, complete, direct, unshared responsibility as against collective, limited, indirect, shared responsibility. Where something in particular is done, it is done by somebody in particular. A gang of youths may incite each other to violence. If our concern is with who actually struck the blow, then the answer does need to be in terms of an individual or individuals. We do, of course, have this concern. The answer to this, however, is not the answer, in any important sense, to the question of who is responsible. In deciding who is responsible in the sense of who is to be blamed, we will certainly want to go beyond the discovery of who actually wielded the club or the knife. The blow may have been struck by the weakest and most easily led of the gang, goaded into it by some of the more cunning or more cowardly of the others. In such circumstances we might well want to say that a greater degree of responsibility lay with those who incited to than with those who actually performed the act of violence. Or we might say that the element of indirect responsibility is here of at least as great importance as that of direct responsibility. Or (though this would be to make a somewhat different point) we might hold that the notion of collective responsibility should apply here instead of, or as well as, that of individual responsibility.

The analysis of responsibility used to be seen as a matter chiefly of isolating one or two positive features. Apart from the difficulties already mentioned, this kind of approach commonly involves a concentration on actions apart from their consequences. Yet when we ascribe responsibility it is often not for a man's actions so much as for their consequences. It would be odd to say 'When I perform the action of swatting a fly I am responsible for swatting the fly' (odd because the second half of the sentence seems to do little more than repeat in other words what is said in the first half). It would not, however, be odd to say, 'I am responsible for the death of that fly because it was I who swatted it.' What I am responsible for is killing the fly, but my action was the swatting of the fly. What I am held to be responsible for is not so much what I did in itself as what has come about through my doing it. We need also to note that what we choose to call an action can be limited to something very brief in duration or it can be seen as extending over quite a long period. This also bears upon what is involved in the ascription of responsibility. Consider the case of someone visiting a lonely old person in order to cheer her up. This is the sort of thing that we should describe as a kind action, but the 'action' here may last a fairly long time – unless we are going to say, not very plausibly, that it consists simply in going along to visit her, not in being there. Such an action could, no doubt, be split up into 'sub-actions': the action of smiling, of shaking hands, of moving the old person's chair nearer the fire, of listening sympathetically, of saying 'How are you feeling today?', of saying scores of other things. But to split it up in this way would be misleading. When we praise the visitor for his kind action we are not praising him for opening a door, and for saying certain words, and for moving the chair nearer the fire – not even for listening sympathetically. We are praising him for the visit. What is he 'responsible' for? One thing and many things. He is responsible for making the visit, and responsible for some of the things that take place during the visit. It is possible, however, that he should be in a sense not responsible for many of these more specific things (suppose he moved the chair nearer to the fire by mistake, suppose everything he said he said without thinking, and so on); and yet he may still be held responsible for the kind action of making the visit – or, more likely, in the light of what we have just noted about consequences, for the happiness the visit has brought to the old woman.

The traditional approach has the double fault of being over-positive and over-simple. It is natural to suppose that where there is a pair of terms like 'responsible' and 'irresponsible' (or 'non-responsible' or 'not responsible') the first of them stands for some one positive property and the second for its absence. Yet on examination it sometimes turns out that this is not the case. J. L. Austin argued in this way about the terms 'real' and 'unreal': being a real duck is a matter of not being an unreal one, that is, variously and in the appropriate circumstances, not a decoy duck, not a stuffed duck, not a hallucination of a duck, not . . . etc.; 'the function of "real" is not to contribute positively to the characterization of anything, but to exclude possible ways of being *not* real' (Austin (2), pp. 67–71). Similarly, when a man is responsible for an action this may seem that certain things are not the case, what things again depending upon the circumstances; that he was not forced at pistol point, that he was not drunk when he did it, that it was not an accident, etc. Austin presented some such view as this (Austin (1), pp. 123–152); and so has Hart, though he has since withdrawn somewhat from this position (Hart (4), Preface). Hart has developed the implications of saying that responsibility, in the legal sense, is a defeasible concept (Hart (1)).

This, as opposed to the 'positive', simple, traditional approach, is a 'negative' and complex view. There is no single, simple property or pair of properties possessed by all responsible actions. To say that a man is responsible for an action is to say that some among a wide range of possible explanations fail to apply in the case of him or it. In practice we are never concerned with more than a few of these possibilities. The negative and complex approach, naturally, has little use for the notion of *the* responsible action, as if all responsible actions formed a simple class and were to be described in the same terms. Most of the range of explanations (excuses, extenuating circumstances) will not be relevant in a given case; there may simply be no question of compulsion, say, or of accident. What we mean by calling someone responsible will vary from case to case (see Austin (1), pp. 123–152).

The best defence against the ascription of responsibility is no doubt to deny that one did anything at all, provided this can be established; successful denial of responsibility in the causal sense at the same time effects an escape from responsibility where this involves blame. Failing this, one can plead that although one did something it was not *that*. ('I didn't say "You silly old idiot"; I said "Pass the biscuits".') Better still, the blame can be put on to someone else. ('I did cause the vase to fall but I couldn't help it; someone pushed me.') If there is no other person to be blamed, perhaps some thing can be – the bad light, the wind that blew me, the stone that tripped me up, my tiredness, a 'mental blackout'. When a man is judged not to be responsible for what he is saying, it may be for many reasons: he is ill, overwrought, very happy, very sad, in love, angry, drunk, and so forth. It is by following up such defences against the ascription of responsibility that we can best come to understand the concept of responsibility.

What defences are acceptable in a given society, and therefore what it means to be responsible in that society, are socially determined. Baroness Wootton has pointed out that with the coming of acceptance of kleptomania as an illness, the kleptomaniac has acquired social rôle, and what was formerly seen as motiveless behaviour is now supposed to be explained. 'I couldn't help taking them. You see, I'm a kleptomaniac.' (See Wootton, p. 234-5.) This was not always an acceptable defence against a charge of theft. It is not always acceptable today; but there is a tendency in this direction. One of the ways in which societies change is in the things people are disposed to accept as excuses from one another — both in the moral and in the legal spheres. The traditional view reflects a society that stood by the concept of individual responsibility and saw little need to extend it. We have noted in a previous chapter the effect on our thinking of some of Freud's views. The reasons why people do what they do are varied. Sometimes they are aware of the motives from which they act; sometimes they are not. This clearly bears very directly upon the question of what we mean when we call an action responsible. Are actions performed from unconscious motives to be classed as responsible or not? This question would not have occurred to anyone before the popularization of Freud's views. In other societies, in the past, the notion of collective responsibility was more naturally assumed than it is in ours now: the meaningfulness of the notion of family guilt is assumed in the story of Oedipus.

The social dependence of responsibility is seen most clearly in the debates about criminal responsibility. In deciding whether someone ought to be punished for committing a certain action we need to consider how far he is to be held responsible for what happened. Was his mental condition, perhaps, such that he could not help doing what he did? Did he act under provocation? Was it an accident? The seriousness of this debate, and perhaps its very possibility, reflects a kind of outlook and a set of interests that mark off our own society from those of many other times and places.

The debate about criminal responsibility can be paralleled in the sphere of moral responsibility. However, in the latter case, it is a quieter debate. No doubt there is not the same incentive here to public controversy, and this for at least two reasons. In the first place, the thing that is most likely to happen to a man on whom an adverse moral judgment has been passed by society is merely that his neighbours will frown on him. There is no moral machinery for locking him up or fining him. The problem of moral responsibility is there-

F

fore apt to seem less urgent than that of criminal responsibility. In the second place, people seem to be tongue-tied when moral questions are at issue. Perhaps this has something to do with the view that morality is somehow a 'private' matter, whereas the law is nothing if not public. At any rate, whatever the reasons, discussion of the limits of moral responsibility, which in principle could well be as extensive and as animated as that of the limits of legal or criminal responsibility, in practice is less so.

Interest in the limits of responsibility, in where to draw the line between the responsible and the non-responsible, has received considerable impetus from attempts to eliminate the distinction altogether. Now that our understanding of human psychology and of society is so much in advance of our forefathers', it is sometimes said, we see that their insistence on individual responsibility was mistaken: the truth is that none of us is really responsible for what he does. Not everyone would take recognition of advances in the understanding of man in society as far as this. This is, however, the direction in which some wish to move, and some certainly think that they have reached their goal already. The M'Naghten Rules, laid down in *Regina* v. *M'Naghten*, 1843, provided a formula used widely ever since to determine legal responsibility (apart from in cases now excepted by the Homicide Act of 1957). A man is held to be responsible for his actions unless he was suffering from a disease of the mind such that he did not know the nature of the act he was committing, or such that if he did know what he was doing he did not know that it is wrong. It is generally objected nowadays to the M'Naghten Rules that they take account only of the cognitive element. They take account of what the accused knows, but not, for instance, of what he feels. A man may know what he is doing and know that it is wrong, and yet be unable to help himself. *Crimes passionels* may be of this kind. Social or economic pressures can also exert an influence upon people's actions of a kind that we are sometimes prepared to call 'irresistible'.

The emphasis that the M'Naghten Rules put upon knowledge is reminiscent of something much older. Socrates held that virtue is knowledge, vice ignorance; that if a man really knows what is right he will do it, and if he does what is wrong it must be because he does not really know that it is wrong. This is an attractive doctrine. The response to it that says, in effect, that Socrates simply failed to see that there is such a thing as weakness of will, is guilty of not taking Socrates seriously enough. There may be such a thing as weakness of will, though it is not altogether easy to define what it is (see Matthews). But it is also the case that very often — though not always — virtue is knowledge, vice ignorance. If a man really knows that something is right he is likely to do it; if a man does wrong it may be because he did not really know it to be wrong. But the cognitive emphasis which the M'Naghten Rules of the early nineteenth century share with the philosophy of the Ancient Greeks has come to seem too strong. Emotional and social factors need also to be taken into account in the ascribing of responsibility for action. To these is often added considerations about free will, or rather the supposed lack of it: free choice is an illusion, it is sometimes said; therefore men are never responsible for their actions.

What are we to say of all this? Is it the case that we can dispense with the concept of responsibility? Undoubtedly it is right to extend the category of the non-responsible at the expense of that of the responsible. The M'Naghten Rules are too narrow. On the other hand, the dividing line can hardly be moved so far that it reaches the very edge of the whole class of actions; for then it would no longer function as a dividing line. There is little point in saying that we are responsible for none of our actions. To be able to say of some actions that they are non-responsible we need to be able to contrast them with others of which we are prepared to say that they are responsible. Undoubtedly, many of those who maintain that we are not responsible for any of our actions want to mean by this that we are not responsible for them in the same sense as that in which others would say that we are not responsible for certain actions by contrast with certain others for which we are. But there is little point in using 'non-responsible' if we deny applicability to 'responsible'.

Further, we cannot do without the concept of responsibility if we want to be able to distinguish between people we would be prepared to employ as baby-sitters and people we would not. We need not, of course, use the word 'responsible' in order to do this; other words and phrases would do just as well: but whatever words we use, the distinction we should be drawing would be that which we at present most naturally draw by using the words 'responsible' and 'irresponsible'. To show that we can get along without using certain words is not to show that we can get along without the concepts of those words express. We cannot, then, do without the concept of responsibility in the first of the two senses we originally distinguished — where a responsible person is one with a certain character trait or group of traits. We could hardly survive unless we were able to indicate the distinction between the habitually unpunctual, dishonest and deceitful, and their opposites; and this is separate from the question of what we think about people's responsibility for their actions.

Equally, we should not be able to do without the causal sense of responsibility. It is necessary to be able to say whether people have or have not done something. Again, we are not limited to the word 'responsible' for saying this. Nevertheless, whatever words we use to say it we shall be saying what we now say when we remark of someone, in the causal sense, that he is, or was, responsible for something.

What, now, of the sense of responsibility implied in a remark like 'I shall hold you responsible'? Unless each individual is to do everything for himself there will often be a need for one man to entrust tasks to another, and for the other to answer for their being done.

Again, it is difficult to see how we could get along unless we were allowed to mention extenuating circumstances. The advocate of dispensing with responsibility seems to be committed to the unimportance of extenuating circumstances. For him, it is as if there were always extenuating circumstances. But to say that there are always extenuating circumstances is like saying that extenuating circumstances do not count. If we are assured that they will always be there we need not take notice of them. In particular, we need not bother to classify them — into accident, mistake, inadvertance, duress, and so on. Yet accidents do happen — people drop things, or trip over rugs. People are sometimes compelled to reveal secrets by torture. People do sometimes put their pension books into the pillar-box instead of the letters they have ready in the other hand. All these things are part of life. How can we understand human existence if tripping over the cat, handing over a payroll at gunpoint, striking someone in a fit of anger, putting too many lumps of sugar in our tea, are all to be treated in the same way? I do not mean that they would literally be treated as the same thing. But one important purpose for which we need to distinguish between them would certainly have vanished.

Finally, in the education of children praise and blame are necessary, and praise and blame imply responsibility. Could we educate our children otherwise? The advocate of dispensing with responsibility would no doubt say: yes, we could. And he is right, if for 'educate' we substitute 'condition'. This brings us to what is really the heart of the matter, and it also brings us back to the beginning of the present chapter. What is involved here is a question of fundamental attitudes towards human beings. Perhaps the strongest consideration against the view that responsibility can be dispensed with lies in our attitude towards human beings — as persons to be respected rather than things to be manipulated. We have already come to much the same conclusion in the previous chapter. There are arguments to be brought against aspects of the views which treat people as creatures that only behave and never act, that are never properly to be held responsible for anything they do, who do not have free will. Over and above such arguments, however, as we saw, there is the question: are we content to think of people in this way? If we are, well and good; provided we are prepared to ignore difficulties of the kind we have noted earlier. But I do not think that we ought to be content with this.

# CHAPTER 7

# *Punishment*

FROM responsibility we turn to punishment. Theories about punishment are generally built up around one or other of three main ideas: retribution, deterrence, and reform. The association of retribution with revenge is enough to damn it in the eyes of many, but this association is not a necessary one. Retributivism is intended as a moral theory of punishment, and revenge is an immoral notion. The idea behind retributivism is that of moral appropriateness, of what is fitting, 'an eye for an eye, a tooth for a tooth'. The principle of 'an eye for an eye' seems, however, to have been originally meant to limit or soften punishment, not the reverse; it was intended not as an incitement to vindictiveness but rather as a brake on it. One should exact not more than one eye for one eye; morality requires us to match punishment to crime and not go beyond what is necessary to redress the balance. However, although retributivism is a moral theory, from the point of view of a different kind of morality it may well seem objectionable; deterrence and reform are also moral notions — from another moral point of view, that of Utilitarianism. The notion of 'redressing the moral balance' that lies behind many versions of retributivism can certainly be questioned: are good and evil some kind of stuff, quantifiable and moveable from place to place?

Retributivism has the virtue that it links punishment with justice in a particularly clear way. It sees guilt as a necessary condition for punishment. There can be no question, from a retributivist point of view, of punishing the innocent. It has often been suggested that an approach based on deterrence need not be so scrupulous. This charge is not altogether a fair one: and certainly (as we noted in Chapter 4) if punishment is seen to be arbitrarily meted out to innocent and guilty

78

alike it will probably have less of a deterrent effect. Nevertheless, it is clear that retributivism, looking as it does to the present and past and not at all to the future, and seeing punishment as an answer to guilt and not as a means to the bringing about of any new state of affairs, is not open to this objection. A charge which can with more plausibility be brought against it is that it denies the possibility of forgiveness, or that it involves holding that there is a positive duty to punish. The charge here is really a double one, though the two parts are closely connected. It depends upon interpreting retributivism as maintaining that guilt is not only a necessary condition for punishment but both a necessary and a sufficient condition; and there is no doubt that many retributivists do take up this position. That is to say, they hold not merely that only the guilty (and not the innocent) may be punished but also that if a man is guilty he must be punished. There does seem to be something immoral (certainly unchristian) about a view which entails the impossibility of forgiveness and which imposes on certain persons a positive duty to inflict unpleasantness on others — even, it may be, to the extent of working the machinery that will destroy another man's life. It is one thing to pass sentence on a man, another to be the person who actually has to carry it out. There may be a kind of moral appropriateness about matching punishment to crime; but is it not also moral, at least sometimes, to forgive those who have wronged you, and is it not in conflict with morality to require of some men that they should inflict pain on others? However, it is possible to construct a version of retributivism that avoids this objection. Where punishment has taken place the retributivist claims that it is justified by the guilt of the person punished. But this claim, it could be said, does not commit him to saying that wherever there is guilt punishment must always take place. He can consistently maintain that we ought where we can to forgive the guilty, but that when we find we cannot, we need no further justification for punishing them than the fact that they are guilty. This, admittedly, would be a watered-down kind of retributivism; but it is recognisably still a retributivist theory.

Reform and deterrence are the main ingredients of the Utilitarian approach to punishment. Punishment is seen as in itself an evil, not a good as by the retributivist, and therefore as needing justification in terms of some good which is considered to come out of it. If punishment makes the criminal a better man, or if it has the effect of deterring others from committing the same crimes, then the social consequences of punishment are good and may be thought to outweigh the evil of the punishment itself. If it were established that the good achieved by punishment did not after all outweigh the evil of inflicting it, or if some other way were found of getting the same result that did not involve inflicting unpleasantness on people (for example, rewarding criminals instead of punishing them), the Utilitarian would, other things being equal, gladly relinquish punishment as a means of social control.

One of the difficulties about the discussion of punishment is that rival theorists do not always have the same ideas about what a justification of punishment is attempting to do. We can distinguish, for instance, between the justification of the institution of punishment — of our having such a thing as punishment at all — and the justification of particular punishments — say, seven years imprisonment as opposed to five for a specific criminal tried for a specific offence. We can also distinguish between a moral justification and a practical justification. Retributivism is stronger as a theory about the institution of punishment and as a moral theory. Utilitarianism is a theory about both the institution of punishment and particular punishments, and on the whole is strongest when it is offering a practical rather than a moral justification. Its bias towards practicality and its interest in the particular render it more vulnerable than retributivism. He that takes his stand on results shall perish by the non-production of results. The empirical evidence in this field is disputed. Does punishment reform; does it deter? The answer seems to be: perhaps; or: sometimes, sometimes not. Consider reform. It is important to distinguish between reforming a man by punishment and reforming him while he is being punished. Rashdall made the point clearly: 'Now, of course, it is the duty of the State to endeavour to reform criminals *as well as* to punish them. But when a man is induced to abstain from crime by the possibility of a better life being brought home to him through the ministrations of a prison Chaplain, or (according to a system which is, I believe, adopted in some American prisons) by the lectures of the Moral Philosopher attached to the prison, through education, through a book from the prison library, or the efforts of a Discharged Prisoners' Aid Society, he is not reformed *by punishment* at all' (Rashdall, vol.

1, p.292; the quotation incorporates a footnote). In practice, it may be extremely difficult to decide between these possibilities. Again, how does one establish clearly whether a criminal has been reformed or merely effectively deterred from repeating his crime? Although some Utilitarians would not consider it important to make the distinction — good consequences are good consequences — it is important to bear the difference in mind if one is concerned with improvements in the penal system.

Now consider deterrence. What aspect of punishment is it that is supposed to deter: mere loss of liberty, separation from loved ones, being put to unproductive labour (if this is involved), or something else? This question, of course, cannot be discussed in completely general terms: the threat of a particular kind of punishment may deter some people, another may deter others. It is, after all, the *threat* of punishment which is supposed to deter from crime, and in a Utilitarian ideal world — where the right punishment had been devised for each crime, or it may even be for each potential criminal — punishments would never need to be inflicted at all. The aim must be to approach ever nearer to this ideal, though short of a radical change in human nature no Utilitarian is likely to suppose the ideal to be actually attainable. Nevertheless, from the Utilitarian point of view, as punishment is in itself an evil, we ought to work towards its elimination, and in this process we ought to replace severe punishments by less severe if we think they are likely to have equal deterrent effect. Abolition of the death penalty for stealing in Britain did not lead to an increase in stealing. Countries that have abolished the death penalty for murder have not, on the whole, suffered a marked increase in the number of murders. Imprisonment (which most people would take to be a less severe punishment) can therefore be substituted for capital punishment. There are, of course, other arguments for and against capital punishment: here we are only considering the deterrence aspect.

I have been stressing the practical side of the Utilitarian view of punishment. It is, however, also a moral doctrine, as is clear from the fact that it regards punishment as in itself evil — evil though useful — and in so far as it is evil, something that ought to be, if possible, kept to a minimum. It is difficult to write about either retributivism or Utilitarianism without conveying the impression that these are two monolithic theories each clearly-statable, self-contained, and self-consistent, to one or the other of which social philosophers tend to adhere without question. Nothing, however, could be further from the truth. It is convenient to be able to attach labels to thinkers, but it can be misleading. Not everyone who would consider himself a Utilitarian or a retributivist would recognize himself in every part of the accounts of these positions that I have given here. My purpose at present (and I have referred in an earlier chapter to the fact that this can be misleading) is to discuss in general terms a kind of view, rather than the view of any one philosopher of that kind. I am writing here of tendencies, and nothing is ever as simple as it can be made to seem. However, to the extent that generalization about the Utilitarian theory of punishment is both possible and necessary, it is important to note that it is a moral theory as well as a practical one. Its morality is, of course, that of the end justifying the means. This kind of approach can sometimes be unedifying, but Utilitarianism as I have expounded it is not open to this charge. We have noted that although in theory a doctrine that justifies punishment in terms of deterrence might find itself supporting the punishment of the innocent, this is highly unlikely in practice, as the deterrent effect of punishing the innocent is almost certain to be less than that of punishing the guilty. We have also noted that Utilitarianism regards punishment as in itself evil: it is necessary as a means to a good end, but it would be better if we could do without it. There remains one other aspect of this charge, not yet touched upon. Is it right to punish one man in order to deter another from crime? True, the man we punish is himself guilty of crime; but the deterrent aim of punishment spreads out to include others as well — potential criminals who are to be deterred from becoming actual criminals by the example of punishment of the guilty. Is this to make use of people, to manipulate people? In a sense it is; but the common good might well be held to be an adequate moral end to justify this particular kind of 'making use of' people. Further, if our overall aim is to transform the world into a better place, that presumably means a better place for the man being punished as well as for others.

The two questions that philosophical discussion of punishment has centred around are: What is punishment? and What is the justification of punishment? These may look to be easily separable; and in fact they generally are separated — the former commonly being regarded as relatively minor and as a necessary preliminary to the latter. This appearance of separateness is, I think, illusory. The idea has been that one can, and indeed ought to, first discover what the word 'punishment' means, and then subsequently, as an independent operation, develop some 'theory' about the justification of the kind of action that is called punishment. It seems to me doubtful whether this is a good, or even perhaps a possible, way to proceed. I shall return to this point later.

Let us first look at what seems to have become for recent discussion the received definition of punishment: the Flew-Benn-Hart definition (see Flew; Benn; Hart (4)). I shall quote it in the form given it by Hart, for the (possibly unfair) reason that his wording offers more scope for criticism than the others.

The 'standard or central case of "punishment" ' is defined in terms of five elements (see Hart (4), pp. 4—5).

  (i)   It must involve pain or other consequences normally considered unpleasant.
 (ii)   It must be for an offence against legal rules.
(iii)   It must be of an actual or supposed offender for his offence.
 (iv)   It must be intentionally administered by human beings other than the offender.
  (v)   It must be imposed and administered by an authority constituted by a legal system against which the offence is committed.

This definition obviously fits the retributive view much more easily than it does the deterrent or the reformative views. It is sometimes said that what the retributive view really does is to give the definition of punishment whereas the other views give its justification. This is certainly a neat and simple distinction. But it is too neat and simple. Why should a definition of punishment look only to the past and present (as does the received definition) and not to the future? One would have supposed that by now the notions of reform or deterrence might occur naturally to anyone as defining characteristics of punishment. Mr. Benn, writing as a Utilitarian, says of one aspect of retributivism (namely, the notion that guilt in law is a necessary condition for punishment) that it is 'completely persuasive; and this is . . . because it is a definition and not a justification. Consequently, it need not conflict with a utilitarian view' (Benn, pp. 334). But *why* should not Utilitarian elements come into the definition of punishment, and retributivist elements into the justification of punishment?

It may be that Benn and the others are trying to give a dog a good name. Perhaps the operation they are engaged in is a sort of philosophical de-fusing, or neutralization, or kicking upstairs. To *define* 'punishment' in a way that clearly owes much more to retributivism than it does to Utilitarianism is, in a way, to honour retributivism. What could be grander than to be, to the exclusion of your rivals, set out in front as the expression of the *meaning* of an important concept? But, the honour having been paid, the promotion carried out, retributivism can then be ignored without its feeling offended when the more important matter of the *justification* of punishment is dealt with. 'How can you say we don't appreciate you? Haven't we made you Honorary Perpetual President?'

The received definition, in Hart's version, is unsatisfactory in other respects, too.

(1) There is an ambiguity in 'involve' and 'considered' in the sentence, 'It must involve pain or other consequences normally considered unpleasant'. This may refer either to the intentions of the punisher or to the experience of the punished. Some people prefer being in prison to being outside. The rich do not feel small fines. Does this mean that imprisonment or fines in these cases are not punishment? (Though presumably 'normally' is put in to avoid this kind of difficulty.)

(2) Hart says, 'It must be for an offence against legal rules'. And again: 'It must be imposed and administered by an authority constituted by a legal system . . .'. This implies that, for example, offences against moral as opposed to legal rules, or against parental injunctions, cannot be punished or can be punished only in a secondary sense of 'punishment'. Hart himself does indeed describe the latter of these cases as 'sub-standard or secondary'.

(3) Hart says, 'It must be intentionally administered by human beings other than the offender'. No unintentional punishment, then; no punishment by fate; no divine punishment; no self-punishment. But this is to discourage at the outset the raising of what may be substantial issues. It is to relegate to the realm of the 'sub-standard' what are surely quite common uses of 'punishment', examination of which might throw a light on the general concept of punishment, if there is one.

Why is the philosopher interested in punishment? Partly, no doubt, because the clarification of concepts is a philosophical pursuit, and punishment is one of the concepts that philosophers have traditionally been concerned with. But partly also for more practical reasons. An interest in social or legal reform has sometimes prompted philosophical speculation about punishment — in particular, speculation about the 'justification' of punishment. To ask for the justification of something is to suggest that the thing *needs* justification (though there is a sense in which punishment is also self-justifying, as we shall see); for instance, that there is some doubt about what it is for, or about whether it is the best way of achieving whatever it is that it is supposed to be for. There are implied practical interests behind, and practical consequences of, this kind of inquiry. Should we alter our ways of doing things? Should we stop doing certain things? What is it that we are trying to do anyway? Or is it that we are not 'trying to do' anything?

This practical or social interest is better served if the concept of punishment is not defined in the limiting kind of way that I have been discussing. We do talk of parents punishing their children, and we do talk of self-punishment. To say or imply at the outset that these uses are at best secondary or sub-standard is, even when a disclaimer is made, to depreciate any contribution that they may be able to make to the clarification of the concept of punishment. Benn says (p.333) that we do not feel bound to punish people for breaches of moral rules, e.g., lying. He says this because he is using the received definition of punishment. If, however, we were to take the punishing of children as a primary and not a secondary sense of punishment then what he says is plainly false: lying is precisely what many people do feel bound to punish in children, whereas breaches of law — of many laws, anyway — by children are precisely what many people would feel we ought not to punish. Self-punishment involves a strong moral element; divine punishment suggests supreme power and perfect justice; punishment by fate suggests inevitability; unintentional punishment suggests arbitrariness. These are all real elements in people's confused notions of punishment. The received definition succeeds in tidying up such confusions all too well.

Another limiting aspect of philosophical discussion of punishment is a tendency, hinted at earlier, to treat the standard 'theories' about punishment as exhausting between them the possibilities of justification. This seems to me mistaken. The theories are themselves amalgams of separate elements. Their traditional association together can prevent these elements from being looked at sufficiently seriously each in its own right. We need to distinguish reform from education and from conditioning, deterrence from prevention, retribution from revenge and from hostility. Sometimes this is done; sometimes not. Retributivism suffers badly in this respect. The habit of talking as if there were something properly to be called 'The Retributive Theory of Punishment' is widespread. We find people 're-interpreting' retributivism. We find them asking whether this or that is an essential part of a retributive theory. Must such a theory include the notion of an exact matching of punishment to crime? Is it the case that retributivism requires its holders to maintain, as we discussed earlier, that there is a positive duty to punish and does this mean that it does not allow for forgiveness? But these questions only arise because writers approach the subject with ready-made theoretical classifications. To worry whether, if one is attracted by some aspects of retributivism, one is thereby committed to accepting the whole of The Retributive Theory, is to have a worry of one's own manufacture. We ought to spend less time on the 'theories' and more on the separate points made in each of them — and, it may be, points not made in any of them.

I now return to the question of the relation between the definition of punishment and the justification of punishment. Mr. K. G. Armstrong has written of the logical priority of 'the problem of defining the word "punishment" '. 'Clearly,' he says, 'the logical order is first to decide what punishment is, *then* to decide whether this thing is morally justifiable or not' (Armstrong, p. 476). And this, I think, is something on which writers on punishment nowadays are for the most part agreed. On the face of it, this view may look unexceptionable. It is obvious, someone might say, that a definition of punishment is needed before one can start to consider the question of the justification of punishment. How can one sensibly discuss justification unless one knows what it is that one is trying to justify? But is this so?

I have already said that even to raise the question of justification seems to imply that there is some doubt about whether punishment can be justified. But what sort of thing is this doubt? Such a doubt may well come and go according to what we *understand* by punishment. Coming to see that punishment is justified may be a matter of re-defining 'punishment'. Someone might explain his worry whether punishment is justifiable by saying: 'I am worrying whether it is justifiable to inflict unpleasantness on a person just because he is guilty of a crime'. And he might then answer himself by saying (for instance): 'But, of course, the infliction of this unpleasantness should have the effect of deterring others from committing the same crime and so is likely to conduce to the general happiness; this is what justifies us in inflicting punishment'. Might this not amount to a decision that his original worry was caused by a failure fully to understand what punishment *means?* Punishment is not just the infliction of unpleasantness on a guilty person. Punishment is the infliction of unpleasantness on a guilty person in the interests of the general happiness. Or so he may conclude. (Otherwise, it would be something like what Hobbes called 'acts of hostility'.) Here the justification of punishment and the definition of punishment are hard to keep apart. 'What is punishment?' and 'Why do we punish?' are questions that may, of course, be separated, but there is not necessarily a logical priority of the first over the second. The clarification of the concept of punishment may have to be achieved by considering both together. (The objection might be raised that if reference to some purpose to be served by it is included in the very definition of punishment it would become impossible even to ask the question whether punishment might have some other purpose or none at all. This in itself does not seem to me a serious objection, provided the purpose is stated in sufficiently broad terms. In any case, in so far as this is an objection, similar objections, as we have seen, apply to the received definition.)

This is, of course, only one of the things that might be meant by a justification of punishment. To ask whether punishment can be justified may be to ask whether it has any purpose, or whether it is a good way, or the best way, of achieving such-and-such a purpose. It may, however, be to ask something quite different: not why (with what aim) we do what we do, but rather whether it is right to do what we do. But here, too, it is difficult to separate justification from definition. Those who think it important to make such a separation are perhaps under the influence of the desire to keep questions of fact apart from questions of value. But this is something that cannot always easily be done. 'Punishment' is a word heavily loaded with value. A totally value-neutral account would not be a fully adequate account of what is involved in *punishment*. To call something 'punishment' is already to have taken up an attitude towards it — either *pro* or *con*. The Utilitarian, being interested in consequences, sees the pain or unpleasantness of punishment as justified by what it leads to, and so at first sight it might seem that the natural thing for him to do would be to define punishment so as to include reference to its intended aims. Paradoxically, the received definition, which defines punishment in largely retributive terms, is held by many who are Utilitarians of one kind or another. Or perhaps this is not paradoxical after all. As a matter of logic, anything that is included in the definition of punishment cannot be used in its justification: a Utilitarian definition of punishment hence precludes a Utilitarian justification of punishment. So, if one considers justification more important than definition, and if one is inclined towards a justification in Utilitarian terms, one naturally must begin from a definition couched in the only other terms easily available — those of retributivism. But what this means is that far from the questions of the definition of punishment and the justification of punishment being separate, as is often claimed, in this case the former is determined by the latter. The received definition of punishment, because it defines punishment in retributive terms, *rules out the possibility* of a retributivist justification of punishment and leaves the way open for a Utilitarian one. It is not surprising that Benn should say that 'what pass for retributivist justifications of punishment in general, can be shown to be either denials of the need to justify it, or mere reiterations of the principle to be justified, or disguised utilitarianism' (Benn, p. 327). By his (retributivist) *definition* of punishment a retributivist *justification* of punishment is precluded. I see no compelling reason why a retributivist should not *define* punishment in a Utilitarian way and then give a retributivist justification of it.

I have referred to the fact that the word 'punishment' is not value-neutral. To those who say that punishment ought to be abolished and replaced by treatment, 'punishment' is a dirty word. But to most people its connotations are favourable, and along with this goes the further fact that there is a sense in which punishment is self-justifying.

If you see someone behind bars and ask why he is there, the answer, 'He is being punished', itself gives a kind of justification of his treatment. Part of what we *mean* by 'punishment' is *'justifiable* infliction of unpleasantness'. It is not surprising that it is peculiarly difficult to distinguish definition from justification in the case of punishment.

Perhaps we ought to say that what needs to be justified is not punishment (if it is indeed the case that to call something 'punishment' is usually already to have decided that it is justified), but, more neutrally, unpleasantness or pain inflicted upon people by themselves or by other people or by 'fate', etc. The justifications can take many forms. Utilitarians will look for justification to the aims such things are supposed to serve. But Utilitarians can differ among themselves in the aim or aims they mention. People who are not Utilitarians will consider reference to aims irrelevant. A man need not undergo penance with some aim in view. A puritanical community may (as in Hawthorne's *The Scarlet Letter*) ostracize someone, and if asked for a justification of their behaviour consider it adequate to say, 'She is an adulteress'.

There is no good reason to suppose that there is such a thing as *the* justification of punishment-in-general. (Perhaps there is no such thing as punishment-in-general anyway.) Concentration on its aims, in particular, suggests what is certainly a limited, and is very probably a mistaken, view of punishment: as if punishment were something *designed* to fulfil a certain purpose. Men have designed punishments, but nobody designed punishment. People have been punishing each other for a very long time. Punishment can turn up in any human relationship. Lovers punish each other; parents punish their children; the State punishes criminals. Punishment takes physical forms and it takes 'mental' forms. What might in practice be given as its 'justifications' are various: 'She was unfaithful to me'; 'He disobeyed me'; 'They broke the law'. It will be said that aims also have a place. Of course, aims do also have a place. What I am saying is that aims should be put in their place.

# CHAPTER 8

# *Human Nature and Values*

WE noted in the first chapter that one of the interests of social philosophers has been in the construction of ideal societies: if they have not often gone quite as far as this, at any rate they have been greatly interested in social ideals. This interest is more marked in the modern period — say, from Machiavelli onwards — than (despite Plato) in ancient times. The notion that there is something wrong with men or with society and that it ought to be set right has been strongly held by many in the modern period. Sometimes the setting right has been thought to involve invoking abstract principles — notably those of liberty, or justice, or equality. Sometimes, however, as in the case of Machiavelli himself, the approach is more practical and 'realistic'. A rough over-all classification of these philosophies (that is, philosophies other than those that would defend the *status quo*) would be into, first, those that aim at a total reshaping of society in accordance with general principles; secondly, those that aim at improvements in limited respects in accordance with general principles; and thirdly, those that seek improvements in limited respects by piecemeal or pragmatic methods not involving appeal to abstract general principles. (To complete the pattern, a fourth philosophy, I suppose, would be one which aimed at the total reshaping of society by piecemeal or pragmatic methods; but it would be difficult to find an instance of this.)

The use of the word 'philosophy' for all these cases might be objected to by thinkers who take up the third position. These are likely to associate the notion of a social *philosophy* with writers of the first two types, and might repudiate the label in their own case. Still, it is convenient to consider all these types of thinkers together, and the classification is in any case only a rough-and-ready one. There is certainly no intention of forcing everyone into a small number of moulds totally without reference to differences within each category: and some are classifiable under more than one heading, depending on how one reads their work; not every reader is likely to agree to all my classifications.

Of the first kind of approach (leaving Plato aside) an exemplar is Jeremy Bentham. Though inspired by particular injustices and issuing in particular remedies, his work had an essential unity. His aim was to reshape society in all its aspects — its legal apparatus, the educational system, Parliament — and all in accordance with a single principle, the Greatest Happiness Principle. The arrangements of society were to be tested by whether or not they conduced to an increase of human pleasure and a diminution of human pain. Bentham is a good candidate for the label 'idealist' — where this is used to refer to the pursuit of social ideals — although he might himself not have welcomed it. Someone has described idealists as people who want to make the world conform to the mind. That is, they want to explain the world, or remake the world, in accordance with a single rational principle or a very small number of such principles. If there are awkward corners so much the worse for them: they must be cut off, or, if that is too drastic, treated as if they did not exist. The Greatest Happiness Principle has the virtue of simplicity, though like many principles of great simplicity it has also in some of its presentations the defect of vagueness. Bentham himself, in his own presentation of the Greatest Happiness Principle, offered something that was not vague; it might have been more acceptable if it had been. He aimed at consistency and achieved a large measure of it, but at the expense of credibility. His quantitative approach to pleasure (there are no 'higher' or 'lower' pleasures; and pleasure and pain are precisely measurable) makes his views hardly recognizable as a philosophy of human beings. In any case his consistency was not total. As we noted in Chapter 4, he attempted to combine Psychological Egoism (the doctrine that all men are so constituted as to be unable ever to aim at anything but their own pleasure) with Utilitarianism (the doctrine that men *ought* to aim at the *general* happiness); it is an uneasy combination. (But see Plamenatz (2), vol. ii, pp. 9–10, for an argument designed to show that these doctrines are not necessarily inconsistent with each other.)    Nevertheless, Bentham's aims were impressive, as was his influence.  The notion of remaking society along the lines of the Greatest Happiness Principle is one that contin-ued to inspire later writers — notably J. S. Mill, who had been brought up on Benthamite principles by his father James Mill, Bentham's asso-ciate.  The Greatest Happiness Principle has as good a claim as any to be considered the principle behind the modern Welfare State.

We might also have taken as an example of this kind of philosophy Marx, or rather Marxism.  The reshaping of society to which Marxism looks is complete — it is to involve the overthrow of a ruling class together with its values and the eventual abolition of the 'State'; that is, bourgeois values are no longer to be dominant and the political machinery that kept them dominant is to disappear.  There is much about 'freedom' in Marx himself, particularly the early Marx, but this is not a philosophy inspired by abstract ideals.  It is anti-'utopian': the process is presented in historical and 'scientific' terms, rather than in terms of abstract principles of justice and equality; but general principles are nevertheless, of course, involved — though principles of an 'economic' kind.

Of the second approach — that which aims at limited improvements in accordance with general principles — there are few theorists though many practitioners: those who have taken their stand on general prin-ciples have more often supposed themselves to want to re-make their world in its entirety than in part.  It is of the nature of general prin-ciples that they are thought to apply generally.  However, as I have had occasion to remark already, it is a truism that change must always take place against a background of permanence.  There can be in reality no such thing as a total re-making of society.  The contrast between the first and second of our types of reformist philosophies is by no means an absolute one.  It might be claimed that Bentham would belong better in the second rather than the first and that Plato is a clearer example of the idealist-utopian than Bentham.  Yet even Plato is limited by the need for permanence as a background of change. It is easier to devise ways of changing men's institutions than men's natures.  It might be said that Plato does aim at changing the latter, too — by his system of education — but this would be a misinterpre-tation; for Plato's educational system, aimed at producing rulers or 'guardians', proceeds by developing qualities that are already present in the people who are subjected to it. Like practically all social philosophers, Plato held views about human nature. In his case, an essential element was his belief that people are of three types: as he put it in his myth of the metals, the souls of men are either of gold, or of silver, or of iron or bronze. His development of the theory of the ideal State is determined by this belief. The men of gold must be prepared for the task of ruling. the men of iron or bronze must be prevented from ruling. The educational system is designed progressively to find out and train up to their task the people with souls of gold and to set the others aside. Further, Plato was not limited just by irreducible facts — or what he took to be facts — about human nature. There were also certain social institutions that he did not question — notably that of the city-state itself — and these provided a firm foundation on which to stand while he questioned others. The difference between the first and the second types of philosophy is, then, one of degree rather than kind. Whether we say that a man wants to remake the world completely or in part may well depend on how closely we search for unquestioned assumptions in his system.

The third kind of reformist philosophy, that which seeks to make limited changes by pragmatic methods rather than in accordance with abstract general principles, is often associated with thinkers who are Conservative in the political sense, though it is not limited to these. Professor Michael Oakeshott (in so far as he can be classified as a reformist philosopher at all), with his doctrine of 'the pursuit of intimations' or 'the politics of repair', is a theorist of the third type. He argues that social or political reform comes about not by the application of abstract principles but rather by the recognition and setting right of limited and particular illogicalities or inconsistencies in the social situation. Thus, although the giving of the vote to British women was in fact accompanied by appeals to the abstract right to equality, the proper explanation of how it came about, according to Oakeshott, is simply that this was the logical next step in a continuing process that was going on in any case. Social reform requires recognition of the way things are in fact going, and it works by the setting of particular faults right as they come before our attention, rather than by actively seeking out abuses identified with reference to *a priori* general principles. The abstract principles follow the facts rather than precede them, and men are deceiving themselves if they suppose the contrary. It is not the abstract principles of justice or equality or liberty that bring about social change. Social change is brought about, and meditation on politics throws up the abstract principles. It follows that revolutions — in the sense of cataclysmic changes of direction in a society — do not happen. What may appear sudden violent re makings of society — like the French or the Russian Revolutions — are never as sudden or violent as they may look. The repair may be on a rather large scale but it is still repair and not total reshaping. In particular, it is not to be explained in terms of reshaping in accordance with abstract principles, however strongly some of the participants themselves may suppose so.

It will be clear that the interest of social philosophers in social ideals or in reform is not always of the same kind. Some would repudiate the notion of ideals altogether in this matter, and not all for the same reason. Oakeshott is a very different thinker from Marx; yet on this matter they are in agreement: social change is not to be explained by invoking ideals as inspirational or causal factors. Oakeshott's rejection of this view is part of his general rejection of the notion of wholesale change as opposed to piecemeal repair; appeal to ideals (in the sense of abstract principles) he connects with the former. Marx, on the other hand, has no objection to wholesale social change; quite the contrary. His objection to ideals is to their utopian or unrealistic or 'unscientific' character. Although Oakeshott and Marx disagree on the sort of social change they think possible, or desirable, they nevertheless agree in looking for the explanation of it in history and not in abstract general ideals (though Marx does have views about human nature). Appeal to ideals and interest in reform are not always connected in the work of social philosophers. Further, the word 'reform' itself is not always appropriate. It suggests something more limited than what is wanted by those who aim at completely remaking the world. It is appropriate in the case of Oakeshott, but not in that of Marx.

However many forms that interest may take, most social philosophers have shared an interest in social change or improvement; in the liberal democratic tradition an appreciable number of them have given expression to this interest in terms of social ideals — principles of liberty, justice, equality and the like. As we noted earlier, they have for the most part agreed also in taking human nature as given and in regarding social institutions as what must be changed or improved. However, although they have commonly started, explicitly or implicitly, from a set of beliefs about human nature, there has been some variety in those beliefs. And they have not always agreed on the relation between human nature and social institutions.

To consider the last point first: it is clear that there is a difference between the kind of view which finds human nature intelligible in abstraction from social institutions and that which does not. Hobbes supposed that men are 'by nature' solitary and that society is something set up artificially. He supposed that it was possible to find out what men are naturally, or really, like; and his way of finding out was by introspection, by reading himself, and discovering there 'not this, or that particular man; but Man-kind'. What one thus discovers by introspection is, he thought, man in abstraction from society. The discovery was for Hobbes not a pleasant one. As we have already had occasion to note — in Chapter 1 — human nature revealed itself to him as a condition of fear where every man is at war with every man and lives under the threat of violent death — 'the life of man, solitary, poore, nasty, brutish, and short'. Men, he went on to argue, enter into society and submit to a supreme Sovereign in order to escape from this their 'natural' condition. Hobbes's picture of human nature may be true or it may be false. What I wish to dispute here, however, is not its truth but Hobbes's belief that in presenting it he is presenting a picture of what men are like in abstraction from society. Hobbes himself, like the rest of us, lived in a society; in his case, that of seventeenth-century England. He, like everyone else, was the product of his heredity and his environment. How then could he be sure, as he introspected into his soul, that what he was seeing was his nature (and by implication, as he thought, that of other people) as it was in itself, unaffected by social influences? The answer is, of course, that he could not be sure. The significant thing is that it never occurred to him to ask the question. He seems to have supposed that when an individual examines himself alone as opposed to examining himself in relation to other people, he will see something that needs no reference to other people in order to be intelligible. But a man living in society who chooses to examine his own heart does not thereby cease to be a man living in society, and what he finds in his own heart may well only be accountable for by referring it to social influences. Hobbes saw fear as a 'natural', that is (for him), a pre-social, condition of man; and he saw society as the remedy for this condition. But fear might equally well be the product of social life, and far from society being its remedy, our life in society might be aggravating it. Hobbes's methods do not permit him to distinguish between these possibilities. Reliance on the introspection of a highly civilized social man will not do. If there is any meaning at all in the notion of 'natural', pre-social, man, some other, more empirical, way must be found of establishing what he is like. Of course, it might be argued that Hobbes was not in fact claiming to have discovered what man is like in abstraction from society but rather what social man is *really* like, deep down, and underneath his veneer of civilization. This is, indeed, a fairly plausible interpretation of Hobbes, a writer of sub-tlety and ingenuity to whom it is not difficult to give the benefit of the doubt.

At any rate it is clear from the case of Hobbes (or Hobbes in his most obvious interpretation), and others could have been adduced, that there is a difference between the two views about the relation between human nature and social institutions. I am not, of course, suggesting that it is never possible to discuss human nature in isolation from social institutions. This may be possible. But it is more difficult than writers like Hobbes, or Locke, or perhaps even Rousseau, sup-posed. Yet views about human nature, about what people are natu-rally like, or like in themselves deep down, have very commonly been offered by social philosophers, and there has been a strong tendency for them to see such views in opposition to views about what people are made into by society.

Let us leave the question whether human nature is intelligible in abstraction from social institutions. There is still the wider question of whether it is possible to give a general characterization of human nature at all, whether we think of men as 'naturally' social or 'natu-rally' solitary. Many thinkers, as we have noted, have supposed the giving of such a characterization to be not merely a possibility but a necessity. They have seen it as a necessary first step in the construc-tion of a social philosophy. How, they ask, can there be any kind of philosophy of human beings unless we first have some idea what a human being is? Such an idea, supposing it to be fully worked out, constitutes a theory about human nature. In particular, theories about human nature are a normal component of the kind of philosophy that we are considering in this chapter, those that are particularly concerned with social ideals, or social reform.

As we have noted earlier, Hobbes saw men's natures as aggressive and fearful, whereas Locke, more optimistically, saw men as on the whole peaceable and well-disposed to one another. Rousseau saw them as something of a mixture. Bentham saw them as seeking pleasure and absence of pain. Freud came to see them as having an instinct for death and destruction.

What kind of foundation should we require for such a view of human nature? We may be offered either an empirical or an *a priori* foundation. As in other cases where this alternative is possible, to choose the latter is to achieve certainty at the expense of informativeness; to choose the former is to achieve informativeness at the expense of certainty. But the certainty achieved by the man who adopts *a priori* a certain view of human nature and sticks to it through thick and thin, denying the relevance of any empirical evidence to the contrary (and, if he is to be consistent, equally denying the relevance of empirical evidence in support), is so unfruitful as hardly to be worth having. Philosophical systems have been built on such foundations, but this is a matter on which empirical evidence, if it can be found, ought surely to be allowed a determining voice. The evidence, such as it is, is not altogether clear, but it has recently been persuasively interpreted as suggesting that Hobbes was not far wrong (see Lorenz): it is fitting that Hobbes was a pioneer in the enterprise of attempting a scientific account of man.

Suppose it to be possible to construct on the basis of what is recognizably a scientific investigation some kind of picture of what man is like 'by nature'. What then? What would such a picture have to do with our views about how society *ought* to be organized? It would undoubtedly have much to do with it, but the precise nature of the relevance needs to be brought out. In particular we need to consider the bearing on this question of the so-called 'Naturalistic Fallacy'. This expression (first used by G. E. Moore in 1903) has been applied to a variety of mistakes or alleged mistakes in moral reasoning. The form of the Naturalistic Fallacy that concerns us here is that which David Hume identified in the following passage in his *Treatise*: 'In every system of morality, which I have hitherto met with, I have always remark'd, that the author proceeds for some time in the ordinary way of reasoning, and establishes the being of a God, or makes observations concerning human affairs; when of a sudden I am surpriz'd to find, that instead of the usual copulations of propositions, *is,* and *is not,* I meet with no proposition that is not connected with an *ought,* or an *ought not.* This change is imperceptible; but it is, however, of the last consequence. For as this *ought,* or *ought not,* expresses some new relation or affirmation, 'tis necessary that it shou'd be observ'd and explain'd; and at the same time that a reason should be given, for what seems altogether inconceivable, how this new relation can be a deduction from others, which are entirely different from it' (Hume, p.469).

It is, then, not possible to produce a conclusion of the form 'Society ought to be such-and-such' simply from premises of the form 'Society is such-and-such' (or 'Human nature is such-and-such'). From the fact that human nature, or society, is whatever it is, it follows neither that men ought to do some particular thing or that they ought to refrain from doing that thing. Does this then mean that the speculations of social philosophers about human nature and the investigations of social scientists into human nature are alike irrelevant to all questions about social ideals or social reform? If this is so then a good many people have wasted their time; for marked features of the work of social philosophers have been, as we have noted, an interest in both human nature and social reform and a belief in the close connexion of the two. It might be held that this kind of social inquiry can be conducted very largely on the level of fact. The study of human nature, it might be said, shows what are men's *needs,* and then the devising of theories about how society can be changed is no more than an attempt to meet those needs, without any judgment being made or implied about whether or not they ought to be met. This might indeed be possible. But there is an air of unreality about the suggestion. This is not how philosophers have in fact proceeded. They have unquestionably wanted to make value judgments — judgments about how things ought to be — and their interest in men's needs has been an interest in what it is right or proper for men to have; the notion of men's *needs* is not a value-free notion. Marx as much as Plato had a deep concern with how things ought to be. This feature of social philosophy must be acknowledged. The question is how far social philosophers have been guilty of committing the Naturalistic Fallacy.

Although the concepts of fact and value are distinguishable from each other, it is not always easy to find utterances about human beings that can be said to be always purely, or merely, statements of fact. I have remarked in the previous paragraph that the word 'need' is not value-free. Talk of men's needs is generally not just talk about descriptive features of men; in many contexts we will not be likely to understand talk about needs unless we interpret it as referring also to men's rights. What may at first sight appear purely factual statements about mankind often turn out on examination to be value judgments, or to have values somehow embedded in them. To say of a man 'He is five feet two inches tall' may seem merely to be uttering a descriptive fact about him. So indeed it is, on most occasions. But if what is under discussion is whether or not a man can be enrolled in the Ruritanian Police Force the utterance 'He is five feet two inches tall' may do more than merely state a descriptive fact about him; it may be intended to indicate that the man is being ruled out as unsuitable for enrolment, because too short, and to say it is to imply a value judgment.

We need to distinguish two kinds of utterances in which value may be involved. When someone makes a value judgment he utters a statement of the kind most easily exemplified by 'That is good', 'That is bad', 'That is right', 'That is wrong'. Our vocabulary for making value judgments is, of course, not so impoverished that we are limited to one of these four possibilities. There are many variations possible on these themes and given an appropriate context practically any adjective (and not just adjectives) could be used in the making of a value judgment. If we are searching through a pile of books for particularly small ones to put on a small shelf then the utterance 'Ah, that's a small one!' does more than state a descriptive fact about the book it refers to. To say this is, in this particular context, also to make (or better: imply) a value judgment. It is to characterize the book as a suitable one, one good for the purpose; it is to assign a sort of merit to it. The kind of utterance which either explicitly or by implication places some mark of merit or demerit upon something is that which we usually think of when we think of value judgments. But there is another kind of utterance involving values. Some words and expressions seem to have a reference to human relationships such that an adequate analysis of their meaning commonly involves mention of, for example, rights and obligations. 'Father' is a case in point. To refer to a person as a father (more so as *my* father) is not merely to mention a biological fact about him. To say that someone is a father is to imply that a special kind of relationship holds between him and certain other persons, a relationship that cannot be fully explained unless we are prepared to make reference to relations of rights and obligations holding between him and them. A father ought to be respected by his children; this is part of what is usually meant by saying that someone is a father. Questions of right and wrong, of duties or obligations, are involved in the full understanding of the concept *father*. To say this is to say that values are involved. The sense in which they are involved, however, is quite different from the sense we noted previously. That values are involved in the understanding of the concept *father* is a different matter from the point about making value judgments. To say that someone is a father is not to praise him or dispraise him; we are not assigning merit to him or saying that he is suitable for some purpose. We are describing him, not evaluating him. But values are involved in the description of someone as a father in the sense that an analysis of the concept *father* includes value-elements. Describing is not evaluating, but some kinds of describing involve implicit reference to values.

There are then value judgments and there are statements using concepts to which values are related. Some social scientists have required that social science should be value-free. What does this mean? It may mean that social scientists should not pass value judgments about their subject matter: they should confine themselves to describing, to stating the facts. On the other hand, when they thus describe they are almost certain to use concepts — like that of *father* — whose analysis involves some reference to values. Does this then mean that it is impossible for social science to be value-free? This has been argued (see MacKenzie). It seems likely, however, that an argument to this effect gets its plausibility from a failure to distinguish adequately the two senses in which values may be involved in utterances. If to claim that social science ought to be value-free means that social scientists ought not to pass value judgments on their subject matter, the fact that in describing society they cannot avoid using concepts requiring reference to values in their analyses does not effect this. Probably no discourse about human beings can ultimately avoid using such concepts; but this has nothing to do with the other, simpler sense in which it is required that social science should be value-free.

Let us return to the Naturalistic Fallacy. When our subject is human beings we cannot get very far in our discourse if we insist on limiting ourselves to statements involving no concepts which require reference to values in their analysis. Values are embedded in certain social concepts. From what are apparently purely factual statements about human beings conclusions involving values are sometimes properly to be drawn. The reason for this is that there is already a value-element in those factual statements. 'He is my father; therefore I ought to respect him' (or for that matter 'He is a fellow-human; therefore I ought not to exploit him') is arguably a valid piece of reasoning. Being my father, or a fellow human being, is not 'merely' a fact about a person. To understand adequately what is meant by his being my father or a fellow human being is also to understand that he ought to be respected or that he ought not to be exploited. Conclusions about how society ought to be organized can sometimes legitimately be drawn from premisses about how society is organized. Equally they can sometimes be drawn from premisses about human nature. The Prince of Wales's recognition in the Depression that unemployed miners were in need led him to say that something must be done. This was a logically justifiable conclusion for him to have drawn. Of course, even although it could be argued that 'something must be done' (i.e., something to relieve their need) is a legitimate inference from 'These men are in need', that some particular thing should be done cannot be directly inferred. There may be many ways in which a need can be met. To arrive at one of these ways in preference to others requires more than logic. The fact remains, however, that some sorts of apparently factual premisses can lead to conclusions in the form of value judgments. The values are there in the beginning, embedded in the facts. This is a fairly common feature of our talk about human nature and about society.

Another reason why social philosophers are not guilty of a wholesale committing of the Naturalistic Fallacy is that they seldom in fact argue explicitly straight from *is* to *ought*. They proceed on the vaguer assumption that *is* is somehow relevant to *ought*. The defenders of the view that there is a sharp gulf between *is* and *ought* may be inclined to maintain that facts are never relevant to values; that the facts may be of whatever kind and that logically this has nothing to do with our decisions about what ought or ought not to be done. But an extreme position of this kind would be hard to defend. The sharp distinction between *is* and *ought* is intended as an elucidation of the logic of moral discourse. But how do people in fact argue on moral matters? They certainly do not assume that how the facts are has nothing whatever to do with what ought to be done. I do not pretend that it is a simple matter to explain the nature of the relevance of *is* to *ought*. Fortunately we do not have to explain it here. What is important for our purposes is the general point that the logic of moral discourse requires a recognition that we do treat facts as relevant to our own judgments about what ought or ought not to be done. In trying to convince someone to share our moral point of view about some situation one of the methods we commonly adopt is to call his attention to the facts of the situation. One reason why this seems a good thing to do may well be because, as we have noted, values are often embedded in the facts: thus, by calling attention to certain facts, or by expressing certain facts in a particular way, we are underlining — because in a sense restating — our own value-reaction. If someone accepts certain facts of the situation as important, and even more if he accepts our way of stating those facts, he is half-way to agreeing with us on what ought to be done. But it is not just value-loaded facts that may strike us as relevant. For instance, a man's financial circumstances, or our beliefs about them, may be relevant to whether we ought to press him for a contribution to some charity. The number of his children or the state of his garden are relevant to whether we think it right to ask him to help in some voluntary service. It is true that there is no direct jump from such factual premises to conclusions in terms of value judgments; but this is not to say that there is no relevance of such premisses to such conclusions. What is likely to happen is that the link is made through different value judgments. That a man's garden is neglected is certainly not a sufficient reason for our concluding that we ought not to ask him to help in voluntary work. But that his garden is neglected is one fact — together with such others as that his neighbours' good opinions of him are important to his peace of mind — that might lead us to say that he ought to spend his spare time in putting it in order. The judgment that he ought to do this is clearly in conflict with the judgment that he ought to devote his spare time to voluntary service; and we must somehow make a choice between them.

The recognition that facts are relevant to values was obscured for a time because of the influence of Moore's attack on the Naturalistic Fallacy. One of the victims of Moore's attack was Mill, who had written: 'The only proof capable of being given that an object is visible, is that people actually see it. The only proof that a sound is audible, is that people hear it: and so of the other sources of our experience. In like manner, I apprehend, the sole evidence it is possible to produce that anything is desirable, is that people do actually desire it. If the end which the utilitarian doctrine proposes to itself were not, in theory and in practice, acknowledged to be an end, nothing could ever convince any person that it was so' (Mill, pp. 32-3). The objection made by Moore, and by others following him, was that Mill is here clearly mixing up fact and value. In particular, the parallel that Mill draws between visibility or audibility and desirability has been ridiculed; it has indeed been called 'grotesque'. 'Visible' means 'able to be seen', 'audible' means 'able to be heard'. But 'desirable' does not mean 'able to be desired': it means (it is claimed) 'ought to be desired'. Mill, so Moore and the other critics would have us believe, has been misled by the similarity of appearance of these words and has failed to see that they are not at all parallel in meaning, and that consequently any argument by analogy from one to the other must be quite mistaken.

Mill's reputation suffered from this criticism, which if sound certainly shows him in a foolish light. There is no doubt, however, that Mill was in fact making an important point, which Moore simply missed. What Mill is saying is something like this. Just as you will not get people to agree in calling something 'visible' unless it is the kind of thing that some people do in fact see, so there is no hope of getting people to agree in calling something 'desirable' unless it is the kind of thing that some people do in fact desire – otherwise you are being too unpractical. Mill recognizes the need for some sort of social agreement (the need, in fact, for a moral community) before remarks of the form '$X$ is desirable' can usefully be made. There is no point in simply remarking that something is desirable if it has never occurred to anyone else that it is. There will be no response. Your hearers will need to be persuaded, and how will you persuade them? It will not be easy. The difficulty is, as Mill himself was at pains to point out, that 'questions of ultimate ends do not admit of proof, in the ordinary acceptation of the term'; he further said that 'questions about ends are, in other words, questions about what things are desirable'. So Mill is well aware that there can be no knock-down argument to prove that such-and-such a thing is desirable. His position is that we need to start from where we are; we need to begin from what things people do in fact think desirable, things whose desirability we therefore need not try with great effort to persuade them of. His claim is that men do regard happiness as desirable. *Proof* that happiness is desirable is impossible. But the fact that people do consider happiness desirable (as they do not generally consider torture or death desirable) is significant.

The job of the philosopher is not to devise new ultimate ends for mankind. It is to discover what ends men do in fact aim at and seek to understand them better. Mill does not suppose that it is their being desired that makes ends desirable: he is not confusing being desired with being desirable. He is saying that, there being no way of *proving* that something is desirable, the only evidence we have that something is desirable is the fact that men desire it. Obviously, if no one desired a thing there could be no 'evidence' that it was desirable. If men do desire a thing this is some sort of evidence – the only sort available, Mill tells us – that it is desirable. It might be objected that it would be just as good evidence that it was not desirable, on the grounds that the existence of a desire for something shows only that there is something that men either ought *or* ought not to aim at. But the answer to this is clear: desirability and its opposite must be defined in social terms. The concept of the desirable is not intelligible apart from society. Things that nobody has ever desired we simply do not call 'desirable'. We call things desirable if people desire them and we think it right that they should be desired. There is evidence available on the former point: we can find out whether people actually do desire certain things. There can be no evidence on the latter; it is not the sort of thing there can be 'evidence' for. So if we want evidence at all in this field we must be content with evidence on the first point alone; and this is what Mill tells us. 'The sole evidence it is possible to produce that anything is desirable, is that people do actually desire it.' Mill does not say that this is strong evidence, or that it is good evidence. He says that it is the sole evidence. 'Questions of ultimate ends do not admit of proof.'

Mill recognized what Moore and his followers were later mistakenly to deny, that facts are relevant to values. The Naturalistic Fallacy has been expounded with too much enthusiasm and has muddied as much as it has clarified. That there is no logical road directly from facts-totally-without-value-content to values is true, and Hume and others have rightly called attention to this truth. To try to take this non-existent road would indeed be to involve oneself in a fallacy. It is doubtful, however, whether many philosophers have actually attempted the journey. Bentham did; but other writers for the most part expressed themselves with sufficient vagueness to make it possible for them to be excused of guilt by a charitable reader. However, recognition of this fallacy has tended to go along with blindness to the variety of facts and values and of the relations between them. One road is closed; but there are others; and the others are those over which most of the traffic actually passes.

We may take it, then, that some kind of movement is permissible from premisses about human nature or about society to conclusions about what ought to be the case. What kind of movement? It is hard to see that this would legitimize a Plato-like construction of a complete ideal society. Plato's factual foundations are too thin and unsure to provide logical support for an edifice as grand as the one he erects. But, of course, he was not pretending to support his ideal edifice on a handful of facts about human nature. The alleged facts about human nature that he adduces do offer a kind of support for some very basic elements of the ideal superstructure. Supposing it to be a fact that men are of different natures then an ideal society should provide different rôles for them. This seems arguable. But precisely what form these rôles should take cannot be deduced from the fact that men are of different natures. Conclusions of a very general kind can be drawn, but when one is designing an ideal State something more than generality is needed. The precise detail of the educational process to which the guardians of the *Republic* are to be submitted cannot be deduced from a few general points about human nature or about the features of existing society. A quite wide variety of ideal States could be constructed on the same factual basis. If, however, we are not determined to remake the world

H

completely but only to improve it in parts, then a basis in facts may well give us a fairly adequate starting point. Given such-and-such an economic structure and given certain information about a person's circumstances (for example, that he has six children and that he is disabled and out of work) we may consider ourselves entitled to conclude that something of a fairly specific kind ought to be done. It is unlikely that there is only one thing that could be done to meet his need, but factual features of the situation such as the relative ease of doing this or that (e.g., whether it would need an Act of Parliament or merely the executive decision of an individual) will narrow down the possibilities.

A further point needs to be made. If values are sometimes linked with facts then it seems that they are not arbitrary. There is, as we have noted, a tendency among students of the social sciences to wonder whether they ought to make value judgments. This is sometimes accompanied by the belief that the making of value judgments is a 'subjective' thing; that is, that it is no more than the expression of arbitrary preferences. There is, however, nothing necessarily arbitrary about the passing of value judgments. Indeed, on the contrary, a value judgment that cannot be backed up and defended is generally not worth making. No doubt there are people who habitually express preferences for which they can give no reason. But not everyone is like this; and it would be quite mistaken to rule out all expressions of preference as 'irrational'. We have earlier noted Mill's point that although questions of ultimate ends do not admit of proof there may nevertheless be some kind of evidence for judgments about ultimate ends — evidence that consists in finding a factual basis for them. It is sometimes said that men may dispute endlessly about values but there is no arguing about facts. But if the position developed earlier in this chapter is sound, it may be that there is an end to dispute about at least some questions of value also, for precisely the same reason that there is no arguing about facts — that is, because some value judgments have a kind of foundation in fact.

Quite apart from this, there is another way in which value judgments can be supported. Mill's concern was with value judgments about ultimate ends, but not all value judgments are of this kind; indeed, very few of them are. Value judgments of a less ultimate kind can be, and are, supported by appeal to ultimate ends. If the Greatest

Happiness Principle is our ultimate, then judgments of a relatively limited kind, about the goodness or badness, rightness or wrongness, of this or that, can be backed up by appeal to the Greatest Happiness Principle. That this principle itself cannot be supported by appeal to yet another principle more ultimate than itself does not make the process of appealing to it an irrational one. Of course, there is much disagreement about whether the Greatest Happiness Principle ought to be taken as ultimate, but this is another matter. Granted that *some* principle is taken as stating the ultimate social or moral end, subsidiary value judgments can be argued for by being referred to such an ultimate principle.

As far as the distinction between ultimate ends and subsidiary principles (or subsidiary judgments) is concerned, the ways in which we seek to support our value judgments are roughly as follows. We try to justify the latter by referring them to the former, and we try to justify the former by referring them to facts; further, we also sometimes try to justify the latter by referring them direct to facts. There is sometimes more agreement on ultimates between people who are disputing subsidiary questions than they themselves realise. Disagreement about values sometimes arises out of failure to see clearly the principles involved rather than out of disagreement over those principles themselves. It also arises, of course, out of failure to state the circumstances sufficiently fully, or out of differences between interpretations of the circumstances. In these cases, arguments in support of one value judgment as against another take the form of making more explicit whatever it is whose inexplicitness is blocking the way to agreement. Of course, the disagreement may remain. The point is that this is a rational way of trying to remove disagreement.

Appeal to ultimate ends, whatever form it may take, is not always involved. Indeed, in practice it probably happens relatively infrequently. Some would even rule it out in all cases as irrelevant. So there are yet other ways in which value judgments can be defended against one another. If a man finds himself in a minority of one this is clearly significant. Morality is shared, and a value judgment that went quite against the usual judgments of the society would to that extent be questionable. Naturally, it does happen that individuals swim against the social stream, and sometimes through their efforts the stream may even come in time to flow the other way. But the onus is on the lonely individual to argue that his judgment is not merely arbitrary. Until he does, it may be not unreasonable to suppose that he is, for instance, saying what he is saying merely for effect. I am not suggesting that the only right value judgments are conventional ones. This would be altogether too easy a way of settling differences about questions of value. But it is important to recognize that judgments about matters of value do not exist in a social vacuum. Social morality is as real as individual morality. We inherit a system of values, and our own values may be largely determined by this system, whether we accept it or react against it in part or as a whole. In general we are not expected to justify accepting a conventional view but we are expected to justify rejecting it. So an argument in support of certain value judgments would certainly be that they are in accord with the views on morality or on questions of taste, etc., that are current and generally accepted in the society or sub-society in which we find ourselves.

There is no one right way of going about defending a value judgment, and there may well be many more ways than those I have mentioned. Much will always depend on the particular question being disputed. But it seems unquestionable that whenever someone has seriously uttered a value judgment it is always appropriate to ask him for his reasons — or, if 'reasons' would sometimes be too strong a word for what he can provide, at least for some considerations in support of what he has said. Of course, people do make value judgments they then fail to back up in any way. This, however, would be a reason for not taking their judgments seriously. By no means all value judgments are of this unsupported kind. We cannot discuss human affairs at all without making value judgments. It is up to us not to make them frivolously.

# CHAPTER 9

# Social Ideals: Justice and Equality

MANY philosophers have attempted to give an account of justice, and in various ways their accounts have been inadequate. Some discussions of justice involve honest over-simplification. We find this exemplified in the beginning of Book I of Plato's *Republic*. There Cephalus says that justice is telling the truth and paying one's debts; his son Polemarchus says that it is giving each man his due, and explains that what he means by this is doing good to one's friends and harm to one's enemies. Socrates in reply argues that such views are too limited. No doubt, as Cephalus says, the just man does in general tell the truth and repay his debts; but if a man who has since gone mad asked you to return a knife you had previously borrowed from him would it be just (i.e., right) to give it to him? Polemarchus's view is represented by Socrates as implying that justice is some kind of craft or skill; and then the difficulty, he suggests, is to see in what department of life the just man — as opposed to the physician, or the cook, or the navigator — is skilled. Further, since to be skilled at something involves also knowing how to do the opposite (the physician knows how to prescribe poison as well as life-saving medicine), the just man must be skilled at stealing other people's money as well as at keeping it safe; and this is paradoxial. Whatever we may think of Socrates's arguments here, there is no doubt that Cephalus and Polemarchus have failed to see clearly enough the complexities in the concept of justice. What they say is not exactly false; but it is incomplete. They have taken aspects of justice for the whole.

Thrasymachus, in the same Book of the *Republic,* is a more difficult case. He is also an over-simplifier, but perhaps not such an honest one. He defines justice as the interest of the stronger, and we may well doubt whether this should be called over-simplification or just plain wrong. Socrates does not dispute with him the contention that justice consists in serving an interest; he disputes only the contention that it consists in serving the interest of the stronger. Again the assumption is made that justice is a craft or skill: but, it is argued, skills are not practised in the interests of the practitioners; the physician exercises his skill in the interests of his patients, the navigator in that of his ship. If ruling is a skill (in the discussion the stronger are identified with rulers), then it must surely be exercised in the interests of the ruled, not of the rulers themselves. The argument with Thrasymachus continues beyond this point, but we need not follow it further.

Cephalus and Polemarchus we have described as honest over-simplifiers. Thrasymachus is harder to characterize; how his views about justice are to be understood is something scholars dispute about. However, somewhat arbitrarily, let us take him as an example of those thinkers who are advocates of a point of view (in this case, that might is right) and who attempt to support that point of view by using certain terms of favourable connotation (in his case, justice) in a biased way. These, then, are two ways in which an account of justice may fail to be adequate: because, without intending to, it sees only part of the picture, or because, fully intending to, it limits, or even deliberately twists, the meaning of justice.

More important than either of these kinds of inadequacy through over-simplification is the following, on which, indeed, it is likely that they depend. The attempts of philosophers, from Plato to Sidgwick, to give an account of justice have been hampered by the fact that they have commonly been searching for the essence, or the 'real meaning', of justice (see Stevenson, pp. 219—226). The trouble with this is that justice has no essence. That is to say, there is not hidden away behind the wide variety of things to which the term is applied something which is *really* justice.

Consider the extent of this variety. Sometimes treating people justly means treating them equally. Not always, however. Where people's needs differ, or where they are in some other respect different, justice may require that they be treated unequally. Aristotle considered that injustice arises when equals are treated unequally and also when unequals are treated equally. In any case, the notions of equality and inequality are themselves complex. The words 'equal' and 'unequal' often carry a suggestion of the quantifiable, so that equality and inequality apply most naturally when something is being distributed among a number of people ('equal shares'). There are, however, uses of 'equality' where this is not so. That every man is equal, that none is to count for more than any other, is an aspect of equality that is not easily quantifiable: it is a way of talking about people's political or social rights, rather than directly about their entitlement to a share of something that is being distributed. Justice does not always involve either distribution or the direct assessing of one person's claims as against those of others.

Sometimes treating people justly means treating them fairly; and this has somewhat different associations from those of equality or inequality. Fairness is linked with non-discrimination. The idea of impartiality is closely related to this, but the concepts of fairness and impartiality are not identical. The impartial man is the man who does not show favour, but this could be in a somewhat negative way. The fair man, we may be more inclined to think, is called upon to do something positive — frequently to set right a balance that has been disturbed.

Sometimes treating people justly means showing respect for them; and here being unjust means being aggressive, riding roughshod over people. The unjust man is the man without feelings: the just man loves and cares for his fellow-men.

Justice on the level of personal relations may take different forms from those taken by social justice (the right to security and to a fair return for labour, etc.). Justice on the international level is different again, and it is a matter of dispute how far the same principles apply.

The notion of justice is closely connected with that of law, but we need to distinguish between the aspect of justice which is shown in the administration of laws and that which is shown in judgments that we may sometimes feel impelled to make about the rightness or wrongness of those laws themselves: a law may be administered either justly or unjustly, but irrespective of whether it is being administered justly we may want to say that it is itself, in another sense, a just or an unjust law.

Justice looks in two directions at once. On the one hand, it looks towards what we may call virtue-in-general, where the just man means the good man and the just State the good State. This is broadly the sense of justice in the discussions referred to in the *Republic*. On the other hand, it looks towards a particular aspect of virtue, where although a just man is always a good man, a man may be good without being just, in the sense that his goodness takes forms – conscientiousness, for instance – to which it would not seem natural to attach the label 'just'.

Very often where we feel it appropriate to call behaviour either just or unjust, in the second of the senses distinguished, it is because we recognise a relation of superiority and inferiority (albeit often of a temporary or limited kind), between the persons involved. Men behave well or badly towards their equals; they behave justly or unjustly towards their inferiors. A father or a headmaster can be just or unjust in his dealings with his children or pupils. It is less natural to say that the children or pupils can behave justly or unjustly towards each other.

Enough has been said to show some of the complexity of the concept of justice. Is there anything in all this that can be singled out as the essence, the 'real meaning', of justice? Equality has its advocates, and fairness, and balance or harmony. It would, however, reflect better our understanding of justice if we were content to say that the concept of justice is a blanket concept, and that any attempt to represent one aspect of it as its 'essence' can only result in oversimplification or distortion. To discuss justice is to discuss many things. An analysis of justice means an analysis of equality, fairness, respect for persons, the law, etc. This is not to say that some sort of account cannot be given of the overall concept of justice; but the point is that such an account needs to be a lengthy one: the 'essence' of justice is not to be encapsulated in a brief sentence. Aristotle draws a distinction between general or universal justice (lawful conduct, which can also be called virtuous conduct) and particular justice, the latter of which subdivides into distributive justice and corrective or remedial justice. Sidgwick draws a number of distinctions, including a fundamental one between conservative and ideal justice. Different writers have drawn different distinctions. Whatever classification one may wish to adopt, it can only be a preliminary to a much fuller discussion of the items classified. Both Aristotle and Sidgwick recognized this.

It is not possible to examine here more than one or two aspects of justice.  I shall confine myself in the rest of this discussion of justice to distributive justice and, more briefly, equality.  Mainly, we shall be concerned with the question of the rules or principles lying behind the operation of justice.

Distributive justice, it is clear, involves rules or principles.  If something is to be distributed the first thing to be settled is the rules in accordance with which the distribution is to be made.  'In the beginning all the world was America', said Locke, writing of what he supposed to be the original condition of things.  The America of his day was a land of vast natural resources and very small population. Where there is enough and to spare for everyone there is no need for rules of distribution; indeed, there is no need for distribution.  Each man can take what he requires from the common stock, and if he takes too much, it is no great matter; there is plenty left for the others.  It is when there is not enough to go round that things have to be distributed, as opposed to appropriated; then there must be rules about distribution, and there may need to be people whose job it is to see to it that the rules are kept.

These rules will differ from society to society, and will depend upon many economic and cultural factors.  Tradition plays an important part in this.  What is thought to be a just way of distributing things in a given society will be determined partly by the way in which those things have been distributed in that society in the past.  How things ought to be is how they have always been:  or so people often suppose.  This is not a bad criterion, at any rate for a start; though we should not be satisfied with it for long.  It does give us something reasonably concrete to build on, as opposed to the more nebulous foundations provided by abstract notions of natural rights or the like.

Traditions change, and in our own day they are changing with great rapidity; so much so that a society, by contrast with others of a more obviously static kind, will sometimes be described as not based on tradition at all.  But however rapidly the process of social change may be it remains true — to say it yet again — that there can be no change that does not take place against a background of permanence; the least traditionalist of societies has its traditions.  In the matter of distribution of wealth or income, for instance, there are at any time certain widely accepted assumptions which are clearly continuous with assumptions in at any rate the recent past. These assumptions are, of course, complicated ones: there is, for instance, no simple correlation of the 'high social status/high income' kind, though such a simple correlation was probably more true of some periods in the past. Professions which previously enjoyed high social status together with relatively high income – the upper ranks of the clergy, for instance – have become depressed in both respects. Bishops, deans and archdeacons are not what they were in Trollope's day; they are neither as much deferred to nor as rich. On the other hand, although domestic service is no more highly regarded than it was in Trollope's day – perhaps less so – it does at least bring in more money. Tradition, then, can provide only a starting point for the just distribution of income: traditions change, and we need to know not merely where we are but also in what direction we are moving. There is another reason why tradition alone cannot take us very far. That things have been so is never a sufficient reason why they should continue to be so. Judgments of value enter in. We have already discussed, in the previous chapter, the relation between fact and value. Values can be associated with facts, but the association needs to be established in the particular case. Merely that something is a tradition does not of itself establish whether it is a good or a bad tradition. So we need more than tradition, though we do nevertheless still need tradition.

The scarcity value of certain branches of a profession, or its links with other similarly qualified people elsewhere, can lead to the establishment of salary differentials. An increase in the bargaining power of some – through organization in a trade union, for instance – can improve their position as against that of others less well organized or more unworldly. Those who benefit by such changes are more likely to call them just than are those whose position has become relatively worse. (There is something to be said for Thrasymachus's notion that justice is the interest of the stronger.) Clearly one would like to have principles which are independent of the interests of particular groups. That some people have improved their position as against that of others is a good thing – for them. Whether or not it is just is another question. The modern equivalent of the Victorian housemaid enjoys better conditions than her predecessor. This is a tribute to her greater scarcity value; but it is also at the same time more just. The modern dean or archdeacon is worse off relatively to other professional men than was his Victorian equivalent. This is a reflection of social and economic changes; but whether he has been treated justly or unjustly by society is another question, and the answer to it is not contained in the social and economic facts. What a housemaid or a dean gets is one thing; what a housemaid or a dean is worth is another. Some would deny this difference and would claim that a man is worth what he can get, and in a sense this is true; but the Welfare State is built upon different principles. From a narrowly *laissez faire* economic point of view, no doubt, a man is worth what he can get, but this is not the only point of view. The man who is unemployable is worth nothing – from this point of view. He is still, however, worth something as a human being, and in a society where the possibility of the continuation of life is dependent upon some money income, such a man needs an income. He has a right to it, and someone – probably the State – has a duty to supply it.

Natural rights (or, as they are more commonly called nowadays, human rights) have been invoked in support of various, and widely opposed, states of affairs or proposals. The expression 'natural rights' is sometimes associated with doctrines concerning the origins of political society and also sometimes with doctrines about a divine source of moral principles. The expression 'human rights' does not have these associations, which is doubtless why it has come in recent years to replace the older expression. 'Natural rights' still has a ring of familiarity, however, and I shall use it in preference to 'human rights'. Men have a right to be treated justly; but this can be interpreted in different ways. As I remarked earlier, a foundation in tradition, where we are after all dealing in facts, may well seem firmer than one in abstract natural rights. Yet, as we have seen, tradition is not enough; and in seeking to replace bad practices by better, men have, not surprisingly, tended to look to the vague and accommodating abstract to redress the wrongs of the all too hard and unaccommodating concrete. Men, it is claimed, have a *right* to a just wage, and, indeed, to a 'proper' share in whatever goods society has to distribute. The appeal here is over the head of the particular society to which a man may belong to the abstract notion of Society itself; or over the head of the moral rules of a society to moral rules held to be binding upon all men; or even over the heads of social arrangements and moral rules altogether, whether particular or general, to God. Men enjoy certain rights in virtue of their membership of a particular society, but many of these are more limited than the rights that the believer in natural rights is interested in. In a particular society there may be a guaranteed minimum wage, there may be strict rules for the protection of property, there may be free speech, and so on. The rights a man enjoys in such a society will be considerable. They remain, however, rights dependent upon the arrangements of that society. Rights that exist in virtue of the arrangements — legal, moral, social, economic — of particular societies are not sufficient for the believer in natural rights. Societies can change, and good societies can become bad. Some appeal beyond the arrangements of particular societies, even societies that happen to be good, is therefore held to be necessary. We need to be able to condemn a whole society because its practices infringe 'natural' rights, just as, of course, we also need to be able to praise a whole society because its practices take account of these rights. If the only sense that could be given to rights was that where rights are understood as dependent on the arrangements of particular societies, we should not be able to do this. It follows that there must be rights not so dependent, that is, what we call natural or human rights. So we may suppose the believer in natural rights to argue. Is his argument a good one? As I have presented the position, the believer in natural rights sees them as rights against societies rather than as rights within societies. There are other ways in which the case might be presented, but this is a useful way. It is sometimes argued nowadays that the concept of natural rights is meaningless, but I am not concerned with this issue. I am concerned rather with the practical usefulness or otherwise of an appeal to natural rights.

Natural rights are vague, it is said; it is not adequately explained what in practice the alleged natural right to justice or equality amounts to. The definition of such concepts is not an easy matter, and I have insisted on this myself earlier in the chapter. Writers have preferred to take refuge in generalities, and it is of the nature of natural rights to be general. Generalities can be interpreted in particular terms if the need is felt. However, the tendency is to impose on them interpretations determined by the social arrangements with which the interpreter is most familiar — namely, his own; and then the virtue of natural rights as rights against particular societies is undoubtedly compromised. A natural right theorist like Locke, who believed that we have natural rights to life and liberty, saw nothing inconsistent in slavery (in the case of 'captives taken in a just war') or in the State's exacting the death penalty for certain crimes. Appeals to natural rights tend to function chiefly as slogans, not as clear principles of detailed application. What we see as covered by our slogans remains to be decided, and in deciding it we are bound to be much affected by those aspects of our own social arrangements that we take for granted. Thus Locke claimed that men have a natural right to property, but he probably interpreted this in a way determined by his own society, a society of rich and poor; and it is likely that in practice the 'natural right' to property that Locke claimed was chiefly a 'natural right' for the landowning class. Assuming this to be so, there is nevertheless no reason to suppose that Locke was insincere. He could not help seeing things as he did. The consequences for natural right theory are, however, serious. That Locke should have seen nothing inconsistent in drawing limitations to the alleged natural rights to life, liberty and possessions illustrates the way in which natural rights can be overridden by what are thought to be necessary social arrangements. All men have a right to life, but they can forfeit that right by becoming murderers. All men have a right to liberty, but the American economy requires that some men should be slaves. Some men forfeit the right to life or liberty by unfortunately being Jews. In practice natural rights are subject to definition or limitation by the arrangements of particular societies. Appeal to natural rights, then, offers little real protection. Whether they confer any *de facto* right on any individual will depend on whether they are recognized in the arrangements of the society to which that individual belongs. If we are looking for rules or principles of justice natural rights have little to offer us — even as pious expressions of hope. How far have abstract principles of natural right actually been the inspiration of social justice? To a limited extent, if at all — as Oakeshott has persuasively argued.

Appeal to a natural right to just or equal treatment, then, turns out to be less effective than we might have supposed. In practice, the alleged natural right to just treatment is subject to interpretation in terms of the rights that particular societies are prepared to allow their members, and (if Oakeshott is right) the historical effectiveness of appeals to natural rights or the like in bringing about changes in the direction of greater justice is illusory. It looks as if, after all, natural rights provide no firmer a foundation for justice than does tradition. We began this part of the discussion by noting that distributive justice requires rules or principles. We have seen reason to conclude that neither tradition nor natural rights can provide adequate rules or principles. Customary principles, to the extent that they are merely customary, do not tell us how we *ought* to distribute goods. So-called 'natural' rights have no real existence apart from what may be allowed in a given State: or, in other words, the appeal to natural rights, though at first it appeared as an alternative to tradition, in the end is no alternative for it leads us back to tradition. We need to look elsewhere for our rules or principles.

It will be convenient now to take up the other aspect of justice that we are chiefly concerned with, namely, equality. Distributive justice and equality come together at this point. The principles that we invoke in settling questions of both these types are the same: need and desert.

That men are equal and that if there are goods to be distributed they ought to be distributed justly are propositions that are unlikely to be disputed — at any rate, provided a clear sense can be given to them. In what sense then are men equal? It is obvious, on one level, that they are actually far from equal. Men vary in physical strength, in intelligence, in the number of their possessions, and so on. It might seem, however, that they are equal in that they are all men: it might seem that what they have in common is humanity. It is not impossible to give this an intelligible interpretation. To be human is, among many other things, to experience remorse; it is to have intentions, to act with the aim of bringing things about. Properly expanded, such facts would constitute some kind of account of what it is to be a human being. But general facts about human beings of the kind mentioned, though certainly relevant, do not give us what we require. We require also propositions about need and desert or merit.

People have different needs and different merits; but to the extent that their needs and merits are the same they deserve equal treatment. Men do not differ in their need for food and drink and for shelter: justice requires that these needs be equally met. This does not mean that they must be met in exactly the same way. Though men are equally deserving of shelter it does not follow that they are deserving of equal shelter; i.e., that they need to inhabit the same kind of house. Principles of justice or equality are not intended to rule out differences between men: they lay down what differences are acceptable. Now, it is true that differences of wealth between men, which may be reflected in, among other things, differences in the kinds of house they inhabit, are held by some to be totally unacceptable. But to others they are acceptable, and are not thought of as unjust. The interpretation of equality that I am adopting here is the minimum one. People differ about whether inequalities of wealth are just, but they do not, in general, differ about whether men have an equal need of shelter. It is in this sense that we can say that where men's needs are the same they deserve equal treatment. Similarly in the case of merits or deserts. Men deserve respect; but although equally deserving of respect they are not necessarily deserving of equal respect.

This minimum principle of equality says very little. But if it said more it would be more open to dispute. Our aim here is not to argue for one view against others but to find some expression of principle that will not need argument at all. The nearest we are likely to come to such a principle is that just stated. But, as is usual in such matters, the penalty of limiting oneself to an unexceptionable principle is that there is not much that can be done with it. That men should be treated equally when their needs and merits are equal may not be disputed. But what of cases where men's needs and merits are not equal? We have already had occasion to note the dictum that injustice arises where unequals are treated equally as well as where equals are treated unequally. Further, who is to be entrusted with the responsibility of saying in what respect men's needs and merits are equal?

It is sometimes supposed that the discovery of differences in men's needs presents fewer problems than the discovery of differences in their merits. The former, on the face of it, seems to be an empirical matter, the latter one of values. But the difference is not as sharp as this. To say that men have certain *wants* would indeed be to make what is largely an empirical judgment; but to say that they have

certain *needs* is to make a judgment with a clear value content as well
as a factual content (as we saw in Chapter 8). To say that someone
needs something is often to imply that he ought to have it; whereas
to say that he wants it would only rarely be to imply this. Whether
someone merits or deserves something is a question of value, but so,
very largely, is the question whether someone has such-and-such
needs.

As judgments of value are involved in both cases, it is clear that
there is the possibility of lengthy and perhaps unresolved dispute on
both questions. Discussion of these matters which assume that the
issues are clear are unsatisfying. The issues are not clear. What
constitutes relevant differences between people − thus justifying
their 'unequal' treatment − can give rise to considerable disagreement.
This is not meant to imply that there is never any way of settling
disputes about such matters. Certain considerations may be agreed
by both sides to be relevant; but the possibility of agreement in some
cases only shows that the dispute in those cases is not a fundamental
one. Within a given society agreement can often be reached on what
differences of need or desert are relevant, but between one society
and another it may be much more difficult, and may never be reached
at all.

The minimum principle of justice − that men should be treated
equally where their needs and merits are equal and unequally where
their needs and merits are unequal − may not give us much; but it
dose give us something. It would be vain to look for anything more
detailed and precise. Detailed accounts of social justice often consist
in the exposition of agreed points about needs and merits, and there
are always some agreed points when the persons taking part in the
discussion are standing on common social or political ground. The
existence of agreement on questions about need and merit could
certainly not be offered as evidence of some eternal foundation for
the more specific principles being put forward. The existence of pro-
found disagreement might equally be evidence for this, provided we
were able to persuade ourselves that our opponents were blind to the
truth. Better still, we should conclude that although there are principles of justice there is no good reason to hold up some of them as
'absolute' or 'ultimate'.

# CHAPTER 10

# Social Ideals: Liberty

LET us turn from justice and equality to liberty. It might be supposed that the meaning of liberty, and the best arguments for it, would be found by considering the contrast between a liberal democratic State and a totalitarian State. This, however, is not so. If men are far apart socially or politically there is not much hope of their meeting on questions about the meaning of social or political concepts. They may use the same words, but what they mean by them is likely to be so widely different that they often cannot enter into useful discussion. It is when men's social or political attitudes are in many respects the same that they can discuss with most profit the differences that nevertheless remain. It is what liberty means in a liberal democracy that we need now to consider, not the contrast between this and what it meant, say, to the pigs of Orwell's *Animal Farm* or the people of his *1984,* or for that matter for a citizen of the Soviet Union today, or for someone living in a feudal State.

The ideal of liberty has inspired both writers and revolutionaries. It is the former that chiefly concern the philosopher. We need first to consider a distinction often made nowadays, that between negative and positive liberty. Negative liberty is what most people would be likely to think of if asked to give a definition of 'liberty': not being restrained, being left alone. Positive liberty, on the other hand, is (roughly) the liberty to develop one's potential. The latter definition of liberty is altogether less likely to occur to anyone in a modern liberal democracy. The kind of liberty chiefly implied in the name 'liberal democracy' is negative liberty, and those who have wanted to recommend positive liberty have sometimes found it difficult to explain what they meant, let alone to persuade assent. The argument that a believer in positive liberty tends to bring against negative liberty is that the kind of freedom offered by the latter is freedom to starve. It is certainly true that the recommendation of an unqualified negative liberty — where people are simply to be left alone and not interfered with — does imply a 'weakest to the wall' attitude. Anyone who should say, in an unqualified way, that people should be totally free from interference would be committing himself at the same time to saying that people should be free from help. No supporter of negative liberty is likely, in practice, to take such an extreme position; but the 'freedom to starve' criticism rightly calls attention to the logical consequences of adherence to a pure, unqualified, negative liberty. In practice, those who have believed that people (in particular, themselves) have a right to be left alone to amass a fortune in business enterprises have frequently also accepted that there is some responsibility on them to do something to help others to survive. Thorough, consistent, out-and-out believers in pure negative liberty are — fortunately — virtually impossible to find.

The supporter of positive liberty argues in some such way as the following. Requiring that children should be educated involves imposing restrictions on both children and parents. This requirement offends against negative liberty. If some children were left to play all day in the street outside their homes those children would be more free than their fellows who are put to sit in school and made to learn things. But they would be more free only in the negative sense. By not being educated their range of choice of occupations when they grow up would be limited. The kind of freedom they enjoyed in childhood would in the long run not be worth having. They would grow up to be the reverse of free — imprisoned in their own ignorance. By submission to the educational system they will have as wide a choice open to them eventually as have the others — that is, they will have greater *freedom* of choice. So the supporter of positive liberty might argue.

The terms used in this controversy are somewhat loaded. It is not his own position but his opponent's that a man is apt to label 'negative'; to call it that is already to condemn it. It is the supporters of what they themselves choose to call positive liberty who have laid down the terms in which this difference of opinion is expressed. The great defenders of what has come to be called negative liberty (such as

Locke and Mill) named what they were defending 'liberty' or 'freedom'. They were not contrasting it with anything but the absence of liberty. If it had been suggested to them that some qualifying adjective ought to be added, supposing them to have accepted the suggestion at all, it is not likely that they would have hit upon the adjective that supporters of positive liberty have supplied for them. They were not defending anything *negative*. They (or at any rate Locke) were defending a right of man. From this point of view 'negative liberty', so-called, and 'positive liberty', so-called, are equally capable of being expressed in either negative or positive terms. There is nothing essentially negative about the one, nothing essentially positive about the other, if we are thinking about rights. 'People should be free to do what they like' is another way of saying 'People should not be restrained or interfered with.' 'People should not be held back in the development of their potentialities' is implied in 'People should be encouraged and helped to develop their potentialities'.

There is at least one important virtue in the positive liberty position, which is brought out by the education example. The example depended on a contrast of some kind between haves and have-nots. Suppose a situation in which *no* children were educated. Then, to that extent anyway, all children would be on a level. No one child would be either more or less free from educational discipline than any other. Freedom must always be seen against a background of restriction, and opportunity against a background of the denial of opportunity; and the freedom and the restriction thus associated should have in some obvious sense the same social reference. There is not much practical point in comparing the freedom of a trade unionist in modern Britain with that of a witch doctor in the Congo. Witch doctors are free or unfree in relation to other witch doctors or other tribesmen; British trade unionists are free or unfree in relation to German trade unionists or British employers. The realization of one's potentialities is a notion that cannot be understood except in a social context. There is no such thing as a realization of potentialities in the abstract. The kind of society we live in determines what we mean by realizing potentialities. (It is also true, of course, that the realization of human potentialities can help to mould a particular sort of society.) For example, it is strictly meaningless to suppose that someone living in a totally non-commercial society might have the potential to be an accountant *in that society*. Again, if a society had no system of reading and writing, it would be meaningless to talk of the reading and writing potentialities of children *in that society*.

It is only where education exists and is socially valued that there is any sense in talking about 'the denial of the right to education' or 'the benefit to be got from education' and so on. Where something exists which some have and some have not, questions about the virtues of being made to acquire it are real questions. Where it does not exist at all, or where everybody has it, such questions are not important questions. What nobody has, nobody wants; what everybody has, nobody wants; what some have and some have not, some want.

The doctrine of positive liberty is intended to correct an imbalance in the 'liberal' doctrine of liberty. It is true that the natural tendency of 'negative liberty' is in the direction of weakest to the wall. But 'positive liberty' is something of a misnomer. The belief that men's lives ought to be directed in certain ways in their own best interests simply is not a belief in *liberty* as this is commonly understood in liberal democracies. This being so, the use of the term produces confusion rather than light. The view expressed by Rousseau that men may have to be 'forced to be free' — that is, forced to conform to the General Will — is not an attractive one. Positive liberty, what crimes are committed in thy name! What is called positive liberty might better be called something else — say, determination, or discipline — leaving 'liberty', unqualified, to stand for 'negative' liberty, defined so as to avoid too blatant a weakest-to-the-wall implication. It then becomes a real question whether liberty is a good thing (it is good in some circumstances and not in others); and there can be meaningful discussion about whether some other value is sometimes to be preferred to it (for instance, security). The effect of calling the doctrine that people ought to be helped towards what is in their own best interests a doctrine about liberty is to weaken the importance of such questions.

We have been considering positive liberty in the sense of determination by society or by the State. There is another sense of positive liberty, in which it means self-determination. A man possesses liberty in this sense who directs his own life in accordance with principles; the free life is the rational life, the self-disciplined life. Both Plato and Rousseau make use of the notion of the free or rational man as the man who is both disciplined by society (or the State) and self-disciplined. For our present purposes we need not consider more closely this second sense of positive liberty, but it is necessary at least to mention it, partly to underline the difficulty of giving a clear definition of positive liberty and partly further to bring out by this new contrast what is meant by 'negative' liberty.

In his essay *On Liberty* John Stuart Mill provides the classical philosophical defence of liberty defined so as to include minimum safeguards against the extinction of the unfit. Mill, unlike Locke before him, does not base his defence of liberty on the notion of abstract right, though he has sometimes been read in this way. He does not say that men have a right to liberty. This would be too easy. His argument for liberty of thought and discussion — one of his main themes — is that it is necessary for the 'mental well-being' of mankind, 'on which all their other well-being depends' (Mill, p. 111).

The general principle which Mill is defending throughout the essay he states thus: 'It is desirable . . . that in things which do not primarily concern others, individuality should assert itself' (p. 115). There is implied in this a distinction on which Mill relies and which has been much criticized, between self-regarding and other-regarding actions. Surely, it is said, there is no such distinction. If there were, then, it is claimed, we could more readily agree with Mill that people should be left alone when their actions are purely self-regarding: but are there any actions that are purely self-regarding; are not all our actions apt somehow to affect other people? It is certainly difficult to conceive of a purely self-regarding action. The case of a man with private means and no dependants, sitting at home engaged in painting a picture for his own amusement, might *prima facie* seem to be a candidate for the class of purely self-regarding actions; but it is, of course, possible that others might be affected by his action. The time taken up on the work of painting might have been spent in conversation with a lonely neighbour. However, the difficulty of constructing an example of a purely self-regarding act is not to the point. Mill is not thinking of purely self-regarding actions. He writes of 'things which do not *primarily* [my italics] concern others'. Our actions are mixed. The distinction between self-regarding and other-regarding actions is not an absolute one but one of degree. There certainly are actions which primarily concern people at large, and actions which

primarily concern oneself alone. There is also a kind of intermediate
case, that of actions concerning two people – or perhaps a small
group. These are not self-regarding, and although other-regarding
they are not other-regarding in the way that those which concern
people at large are. Defence of the liberty of the individual, and
attempts to restrict the liberty of the individual, very often centre
around actions of this kind. Other-regarding acts where 'outsiders'
are affected are fairly uncomplicated, and so are straightforwardly
self-regarding acts. If someone is deliberately spitting at passers-by
then there may be good reason for stopping him doing it. If someone
is sitting quietly alone reading Jane Austen it would generally be hard
to find a reason for stopping him. But consider the case where two
consenting adults are engaged in homosexual acts in private. The self-
regarding/other-regarding distinction seems not really to help here.
Mill writes of whether or not actions 'concern' other people; but the
notion of 'concerning' is a vague one. Some suppose that one kind of
concern only is relevant: the question whether acts are self-regarding
or other-regarding is interpreted as a question about whether they
are harmless or harmful. These notions are indeed part of what
people often mean by 'self-regarding' and 'other-regarding'; one sense
of 'self-regarding action' undoubtedly is 'action that harms no one
else', and one sense of 'other-regarding action' undoubtedly is 'action
that may harm someone else'. The difficulty we may well feel with the
consenting-adults-in-private case is that of fitting it into the self-
regarding/other-regarding dichotomy. It seems to be neither quite
the one nor the other. It is easier to apply to it the harmless/harmful
dichotomy. When problems arise about whether or not to impose
restrictions on certain actions one important kind of argument used
will be about the harmfulness or otherwise of actions of this kind;
and part of what people mean when they talk about self-regarding
acts and other-regarding acts is what is conveyed by the phrases 'harmless acts' and 'harmful acts'.

Mill himself recognizes this as part of the meaning of these terms.
He believes that people should do what they like *as long as they do
not harm anyone else.* But he would certainly not accept 'harmless/
harmful' as rendering completely what he wishes to convey by 'self-
regarding/other-regarding'. The notion of the self-regarding act is not
identical with that of the harmless act. A man may do something which

is both self-regarding and harmful to himself. Such a man, according to Mill, ought not to be restricted. 'The only purpose for which power can be rightfully exercised over any member of a civilised community, against his will, is to prevent harm to others. His own good, either physical or moral, is not a sufficient warrant' (p. 73). If they are left alone men have a greater chance to develop mentally and morally. This development is good both for them and for society. The last paragraph of *On Liberty* deserves to be pondered on. 'The worth of a State, in the long run, is the worth of the individuals composing it'. Unless those individuals are allowed to be individuals and not forced to conform to some type laid down by the State they will not be worth very much. 'With small men no great thing can really be accomplished'. Mill is by no means accurately represented as a supporter of a simple crude negative liberty. His stress on social progress and on the need, if there is to be social progress, for the development of the moral and intellectual fibre of individuals, suggests, if we must use the terminology, as much positive liberty (in the sense of *self*-determination) as negative.

Mill treats at length of liberty of thought and of speech or writing. The importance of liberty of speech for the development of moral and intellectual fibre is obviously very great.. As Mill says, it is by the free circulation of contrary opinions that men become clear about their own beliefs. If you are never required to defend your own beliefs against contrary ones you may lack a strong incentive to make clear to yourself what exactly it is that you do believe and on what grounds you believe it. Your beliefs may be in danger of becoming prejudices, or dogmas. Mental development depends upon liberty of thought and of speech. Mill, rather unsatisfactorily, lumps these two things together, on the grounds that although the latter 'may seem to fall under a different principle' from the former it is 'almost of as much importance' as it and rests 'in great part on the same reasons' and consequently 'is practically inseparable from it'. To say that it is of *almost* as much importance is to praise it too faintly. But the really serious difficulty about Mill's decision to treat these two things together is that this offends against his own guiding principle. He sees this difficulty himself but inexplicably dismisses it. 'The liberty of expressing and publishing opinions may seem to fall under a different principle [from liberty of thought], *since it belongs to that part of the conduct of an individual which concerns other people'* (Mill, p. 75; my italics). But this qualification is crucial. Much of Mill's argument in *On Liberty* is built up on the distinction implied here. It is not surprising that his detailed discussion turns out in fact to be about liberty of speech and writing rather than about liberty of thought; for there is no particular problem about liberty of thought. Who can stop me thinking what I please (brain-washing apart); for who knows what I am thinking? The problem arises when I express my thoughts; for then other people may be affected. But what is surprising is that Mill should here apparently be implying that his own distinction between self-regarding and other-regarding acts perhaps does not matter all that much — at any rate in practice. This distinction is so fundamental to the whole argument of *On Liberty* that we must clearly regard as an aberration this dismissal as unimportant of the difference between liberty of (inner) thought and liberty of (overt) speech.

In a notorious passage in *On Liberty* Mill writes, concerning liberty of speech: 'If any opinion is compelled to silence, that opinion may. for aught we can certainly know, be true. To deny this is to assume our own infallibility' (p. 111). Infallibility? This is going too far, say Mill's critics. If we (being in authority) presume to suppress a novel opinion, we may thereby be implying that we know better. But to know better is not to be infallible. Mill's point is made too strongly.

Thus far the critics. Is this a fair criticism? It seems to me that it is not. Mill's point is not so much that if authority suppresses a novel opinion it is implicitly declaring that it itself is infallible. It is rather that it is because we know we are *not* infallible that we cannot be sure that a novel opinion does not contain some element of truth. This is an important, and true, observation. If this is what Mill means he is far from going to the extremes the critics charge him with. He is rather himself attempting to reduce to absurdity the restrictionist position.

Mill's defence of liberty has been accused of being insincere. He makes a distinction between the intelligent part of the public and the collective mediocrity; and it has been claimed that what he is defending is liberty for the former, not liberty for all (see Cowling). Certainly, Mill thought that educated and cultivated people like himself had something that the working man lacked. So they had; and he could hardly have failed to notice it. But it is not the case that he

looked with any sense of condescension upon the collective mediocrity, or that he was complacent about social differences. He criticized the tendency of the masses not to think for themselves; but he
did not despise this 'mediocrity'; he wanted to shake it up. He did
not want to make everyone conform to the same way of life. The
intelligent part of the public have the duty of persuading others, but
not of forcing them. It is not only 'persons of decided mental superiority who have a just claim to carry on their lives in their own way.
There is no reason that all human existence should be constructed
on some one or some small number of patterns' (p. 125). Mill, like
most social philosophers, was writing a tract for the times as well as a
theory for eternity, and he wanted to combat what he felt to be the
tendency of men in his day not to *want* liberty, not to take seriously
enough the need to make choices. (See Friedman). Our times are different from his in many respects, but they are not so different in this; and
Mill's defence of liberty has still much to say to men who need reminding of the importance of what he called the mental and moral
fibre of society.

# CHAPTER 11

# The Point of View: Marxism

SOCIAL philosophy can conveniently be regarded as a subject lying on the borderline between moral philosophy (ethics) and political philosophy. Many of the topics that the social philosopher discusses – in particular, the nature of social rules, Utilitarianism, punishment, justice – would be at home equally in books on ethics or on political philosophy. The emphases and the details of treatment would, however, be different. For example, the moral philosopher writing on punishment is interested in its moral justification; the political philosopher more in punishment as a social device. Again, the moral philosopher is interested in Utilitarianism as a theory about the nature of the good life, whereas the political philosopher might be more interested in it as a theory about the grounds of political obligation (i.e., as a theory which says we ought to obey the government because – or to the extent that – it helps towards the maximization of happiness). In the foregoing chapters social philosophy has been treated as a branch neither of moral nor of political philosophy, but as a set of themes capable of standing together to form a worthwhile unity. The topics discussed *are* for the most part topics of moral philosophy and political philosophy, but the present book is meant to be neither a book on ethics nor a book on political philosophy: it is a book on social philosophy.

At any rate, the political and moral nature of many of the themes treated is clear, and one aspect of this is particularly important. Whenever topics such as social happiness, justice, liberty, and the like are discussed, a certain question nowadays tends naturally to arise – that of the political point of view. One man's justice or liberty may not be another man's; and some would discount views on these matters on the grounds that they are no more than the reflection of a committed point of view. I believe that most of the topics discussed in the present book are of a kind that can be treated independently of the political views of the person discussing them. But, some would maintain, this belief itself is one that is determined ultimately by factors which have made me what I am and my beliefs what they are. Is it the case that the preceding chapters — with their discussion of such varied matters as the task of social philosophy, the shortcomings of a narrowly empirical social science, moral and legal rules, free will and responsibility, facts and values, justice and liberty — are not what they are intended to be, namely, objective examinations of some central social concepts, but the reflection of a limited and biased, moral or political point of view? This is clearly a question of considerable importance. It is a question about the very validity of the kind of enterprise that is being carried out in the present book.

The sceptical position referred to in the preceding paragraph can take more than one specific form. In particular, it would be a mistake to suppose that only Marxists hold it; the approach of Marxists themselves is often criticized by others on the grounds that they are politically committed to seeing things a certain way. Nevertheless, the Marxist version of this position is particularly influential, and in the rest of this chapter I shall look more closely at it. Not all Marxists are in agreement, and I shall limit myself for the most part to some of the views of Marx and Engels themselves.

For Marx the political or moral point of view is itself determined by 'material' factors. The economic structure of a society is the foundation upon which is built its legal, political, moral, religious and philosophical 'superstructure'. Marx writes in a well-known passage: 'The mode of production of material life conditions the social, political and intellectual life process in general. It is not the consciousness of men that determines their being, but, on the contrary, their social being that determines their consciousness' (Marx and Engels, vol. 1, p. 363). There are unquestionably influences of economic (or material) factors upon other factors of social life, and in stressing this Marx made a contribution to the study of society of the greatest importance. The economic conditions of nineteenth century England may be said in a sense to have 'determined' its literature: Mrs. Gaskell's novel *Mary Barton* was certainly inspired by the economic conditions of the poor in Manchester, just as much as was Engels's *The Condition of the Working Class in England*. The religion and the morality of the Victorians are also to be explained, up to a point, in terms of the economic structure of their society. At the same time, Marx's insight is incapable of really sharp definition or of decisive empirical testing. Marx prided himself on his 'scientific' approach; but a scientific theory must be capable of empirical falsification, and the difficulty is to see in the case of Marx's principle how it can be tested empirically. Victorian England exhibited great variety in its morality, its religion, and its literature. How could the same economic structure — the same class, indeed — produce High Churchmen, Evangelicals, and theological Liberals? How could it produce both socially-conscious novels about working class life and complacent representations of upper class life and values? That it did produce such variety is a matter of record; and this gives rise to doubt about the doctrine of the material infrastructure and the superstructure, determined by it, of morality and religion, politics and law.

If the superstructure is determined, one would suppose it to be predictable from knowledge of the infrastructure. Marx was a historian, among other things, but he did not confine himself to providing explanations of specific past events or epochs; he thought also (as we have already noted in Chapter 2) that he could detect a general principle at work in the past which would enable prediction of the future. That is, he was a 'scientific' historian. But the science is bad science; for the general principle — that of economic determinism — admits of too great a variety of prediction. *Whatever* form is taken by the religion, art, morality, politics, law or philosophy of an age it is still apparently to be seen as the effect of economic determination. But this determination is clearly, in view of the variety to be found in an age's religion or its literature or its art, of a very general character. It is a weakness in the historian, according to Marx, to see the history of a past age in terms dictated by its own assumptions: the historian is at fault if he takes at their face value the declarations of a past epoch about the political or religious motives of its actions. In so behaving the historian shows that he shares 'the illusion of that epoch', as Marx puts it; but he cannot help sharing it. To break through the illusion it is necessary to see that the real forces at work are economic or material. There is no doubt that this has been a valuable piece of advice to historians, and under the influence of Marx history is no longer written as a matter of course from the point of view of the ruling classes in any epoch or as if political or religious motives were the only important, or even the real, ones. The general acceptance of the very subject called social and economic history is post-Marx. But the simple formula about the economic infrastructure determining the political and religious superstructure is only a beginning. Historical study has to be done in detail and in the particular case. The general principle can at most set the direction.

In any case, new methods of production (the invention of the steam mill, say) are brought about through the exercise of men's intellects. It would seem as reasonable to say of such cases that the economic structure is changed by man's 'consciousness' as the reverse, which is what Marx says. Indeed, it would seem more reasonable. It is odd to regard the exercise of man's inventive powers in technological advances as belonging to the material level. Marx seems to treat 'science' as belonging among the forces of production, yet human inventiveness would seem to go better under the heading of man's intellectual life, and therefore on the level of the superstructure. It is true that Marx distinguished between practical uses of reason and abstract uses of it: it is the latter, he believed, that belong on the level of the superstructure (along with religion). 'The philosophers have only *interpreted* the world, in various ways; the point, however, is to *change* it'. (Thus, in the moral sphere, Marx rejects, for example, the kind of thinking that concerns itself with the abstract notion of equality rather than with actual particular social equalities and inequalities.) In general, practical activity is for him superior to theoretical contemplation. Nevertheless, it is difficult to accept a classification according to which human inventiveness goes in the material slot and thus separate from abstract thought — a classification in which it becomes, indeed, part of what determines or conditions abstract thought. It is perfectly possible for someone to maintain, if he wants to, that the pure sciences depend upon the applied sciences; not, of course, in the sense that the pure sciences logically presuppose the applied sciences (for the reverse is true: there could be no engineering without mathematics). In some 'practical' sense the pure sciences might depend upon, or be conditioned by, the applied sciences: for example, the problems actually studied by mathematicians might normally be posed by engineers. Surely, however, the best way of putting the matter — the way most in accord with what actually is the case — would be to say that the relationship is a reciprocal one. Abstract thought inspires practical thought; practical thought inspires abstract thought. The case of science and technology brings out well the point that the determining or conditioning is best regarded as a two-way process. And if science and technology why not morality, religion, or politics? Moral, religious, or political considerations can sometimes determine developments on the economic or material level: governments can give or withhold grants for research; a Church can by its disapproval of some methods of birth control effectively discourage the limitation of population and consequently influence the economic conditions of a people.

The most serious difficulty for Marx's doctrine of infrastructure and superstructure is the following. There are certain conditions which are necessary for the very existence of a society (see Chapters 2 and 3 above). A society cannot exist without language; and it cannot exist without some rules of the kind we call moral or legal. Language is a necessary condition for the existence of societies. A society is not merely a collection of discrete individuals but involves relations between individuals; it is necessary that there be communication: some kind of language must exist. Rules of the kind we call logical must also exist: it must be possible to follow through arguments, however primitive. Some things have to be done by agreement, and there cannot be agreement without a shared understanding of what is to be achieved and how it can best be achieved. Some kind of reasoning is needed. That is to say, language and logic are needed. What form the language takes is another matter. A primitive society can no doubt manage with a primitive language; the ideas to be conveyed could be very few. Certainly, there is no need for more than a few concepts of an abstract kind. The reasoning needed could also be very limited. But it is clear that without some kind of language and logic a society could not exist at all.

Equally, a society cannot exist without morality, to the extent that to be a member of any society implies the acceptance of obligations towards other people and rights against them. In society there must be social rules. We have considered in Chapter 3 both the variety of these social rules — moral, legal, political and other — and the question whether a society needs merely rules or some rules in particular. A primitive society might have nothing that we should regard as clearly legal or political rules, but moral rules it must have, though it could no doubt manage with rather few. In a given society there can be disputes about the acceptability of particular rules and particular rights and obligations, but what there cannot be dispute about is the necessity for rules and the existence of rights and obligations. Anyone who supposed that there could be a society in which there were no rules at all and in which people had no rights and obligations whatever would simply not have understood the concept of society: I have argued this elsewhere (see McPherson, Chap. 7).

But if not only language and logic but also morality (and perhaps even law and politics as well — though this would depend on how one defined 'law' and 'politics') are implied in the very concept of society, how is it possible to say, as Marx wants to say, that human intellectual life — and morality, law and politics — belong to the superstructure and not the infrastructure of society? Even to speak of the infrastructure of society is already to have acknowledged the presence on that 'level' (as on every level) of language and morality: it could not be he infrastructure of *society* otherwise. You cannot have a society, whatever 'level' of it you are considering, without language and morality. Marx speaks of the 'relations of production' as elements in the infrastructure, but for these to be relations at all — relations between people — they must already involve what Marx supposes to exist only on the level of the superstructure. Where there are relations between people, whether economic or any other, there already we have language of a kind and morality of a kind. It is not possible even to state the contents of the infrastructure without assuming elements that are supposed to exist only in the superstructure. The distinction, then, between infrastructure and superstructure cannot be maintained. The notion of the material infrastructure determining, or conditioning, the superstructure containing morality, law, politics, religion and philosophy, cannot be consistently stated.

Nevertheless, of course, Marx's work provides an insight into societies that can be used — selectively, admittedly — to great effect. To look, with Marx, at the history of past ages on the assumption that this or that event might be better explained in terms of the pressure of economic forces than in terms of political or religious decisions, has proved immensely fruitful. Provided Marx's point is taken to be that a particular society, and the politics, laws, religion, etc., of that society, are determined (or, as Marxists sometimes put it — less strongly — conditioned) by particular economic factors, it is possible to get great illumination through it. This has proved an extremely useful doctrine for the historian. Certainly Marx did want to say this. Where his position is untenable, however, is in his attempt to support this attitude to the study of societies by the much more general — and, as we have seen, logically incoherent — doctrine that morality and law *as such* are determined by the economic structure.

The term 'ideology' is used by Marx as a name for a set of legal, political, religious, aesthetic or philosophical views — that is, for the contents of the superstructure. Ideologies are false, they are illusions. Marxism itself, although a set of ideas of a social-philosophical-political character, clearly is not, for Marx, an ideology. It cannot be; because it is true. (In more recent times, however, Marxists have used 'ideology' more widely so as not to imply the necessary falsehood of an ideology and therefore have been able to include Marxism itself among ideologies.) His own ideas, Marx believed, escape the blinkers of other social-philosophical-political outlooks. The bourgeoisie is fettered by its own illusions: Marx and Engels, although themselves members of the bourgeoisie, were not, in their own opinion, so fettered. How could this be? Marx and Engels, in the *Communist Manifesto*, record the fact that some members of the bourgeoisie have gone over to the proletariat, 'and in particular, a portion of the bourgeois ideologists, who have raised themselves to the level of comprehending theoretically the historical movement as a whole' (Marx and Engels, vol. 1, p. 43); but it is notoriously hard to see how this can be so, in view of their own belief that ideas are determined by economic factors and by class. The solution to this difficulty may seem to lie in the fact that Marx thought of his own position as *scientific* and that he thought of science (as we have seen) as itself belonging on the level of infrastructure rather than on that of the ideological superstructure. But there are two difficulties about this. First, even granted, for the purposes of this argument, what we have in any case already seen reasons for rejecting, that a clear distinction can be drawn between the infrastructure and the superstructure, it is very hard to see how science can properly be said to belong on the level of the infrastructure, which is the material level; this point I have made already. Secondly, the influences of Marx's and Engels's bourgeois upbringing remain. For instance, Marx was a student of the philosophy of Hegel, and was influenced away from Hegel in the direction of materialism by the writings of Feuerbach. But this belongs to Marx's *philosophical* development; and it would be hard to explain it in terms of *science*. Marx and Engels believed themselves able to see the falsity of ideologies – that ideologies are held as a result of economic or material conditioning of which their holders are unaware. But it is difficult to discover a clear difference in kind between Marxism itself and the ideologies – the products of 'false consciousness' – which the Marxist repudiates. To the non-Marxist, Marxism itself is a set of social-philosophical-political ideas taking its place alongside others and competing with them for credibility on intellectual grounds; he may see in Marxism certain virtues and may try to learn from them. To Marx himself his own views were 'scientific' and therefore possessed an essentially different character from the ideologies he repudiated.

For Marx the scientific approach is true, the ideological false. A comment on another writer is relevant here. Freud's view of religious beliefs, as stemming from, or determined by, men's inadequacies – their wish to find refuge in a Heavenly Father from their inability to face up to the difficulties of life in the real world – does not necessarily involve holding that religious beliefs are false. Freud sometimes wrote as if he thought they were, but on the whole he did not claim to have shown religion to be false. He asserted not that there is no God, but that the reasons for which people believe in God are other than they suppose them to be. People believe in God because they want to. Perhaps there is a God, perhaps there is not. But the point is, according to Freud, that the real reasons for which men believe that there is a God are not good – are not even relevant – reasons. We all, no doubt, tend to believe what we want to believe, or what it suits us to believe. Perhaps we are often not aware of this as our 'real' motive. But it would not follow that a belief so motivated must be false. Equally, to return to Marx, the view that an ideology is determined by the economic structure or the social class does not carry the necessary implication that ideologies must be false; yet Marx tends to write as though he did think this. If false they must be false for

K

other reasons than that they are economically determined. Marx, unlike Freud in a somewhat similar situation, is inclined to claim too much.

One aspect of Marx's work that I have not yet commented on is his ideas on *alienation,* a concept which appears in his early writings (see *Economic and Philosophic Manuscripts of 1844*). Although he came to abandon the concept of alienation, which was indeed later called by him and Engels 'philosophical nonsense', his views about it have recently come to constitute the centre of interest for many readers of Marx. The term itself comes from Hegel. As Marx saw things, in capitalist society man is alienated from what he needs to make life worthwhile. Man is a slave to the system. (It is an important part of Marx's thought that he did not see the relationship between the capitalist and the worker purely as one in which the former is exploiter and the latter exploited. The capitalist is himself a victim of the system. His rôle is not one that he has himself chosen: it is forced upon him by the system as much as that of the worker is forced upon *him.*) Men are alienated from nature, from the products of their work, and from their fellow men. Men become themselves mere commodities. Men are dominated by the things they produce. They exist in order to produce, rather than because they want to produce, or themselves need the things they produce, or are interested in what they produce. They may be dominated by things in the sense that they are made by the system to acquire more and more whether they need it or not; their lives are governed by 'keeping up with the Joneses'; in this sense men are not the disposers of their own lives. The competitiveness implied in 'keeping up with the Joneses' also ensures that men see each other as hostile: they are alienated from each other. The eventual development of man is in the direction of escape from the condition of alienation. Bourgeois society prevents men from developing as they ought; it guarantees, indeed, that they remain in the condition of alienation.

The notion of alienation is a fruitful but nevertheless an obscure one. Marx associated the condition of alienation not only with class society but with poverty. Class distinction and poverty are both less marked than they were in Marx's day. Nevertheless alienation continues probably undiminished. Men still feel frustrated in and by society (see Plamenatz (2), vol. 2, p. 377). A society in which men no longer felt themselves victims of the system, no longer felt themselves held back from developing their capacities, has been a dream of philosophers and others.  But it may be that the only kind of society in which this dream could be realized would be a very simple kind of society, and the dream might be attainable, if at all, only by setting the clock back.  As things have turned out, capitalism has brought benefits to mankind; certainly it has brought material benefits.  It has also brought great evils.  Technological advances create social problems:  it is a platitude to say so.  But it may be that alienation is inseparable from the kind of technologically and culturally complex society in which we live, rather than explicable by the fact that our society also happens to be a capitalist society; and the cure may lie not in communism but in a retreat to primitivism.  Some might consider the cure well worth such a price.  It is at least questionable how far the kind of thing that Marx seems to have meant by alienation is really the effect of capitalism and not rather an inseparable feature of the modern large civilized nation state, and not to be permanently eradicated as long as we want to retain the benefits that go along with a technologically and culturally complex society.

# BIBLIOGRAPHY

ACTON, H. B. (1). *The Illusion of the Epoch,* Cohen and West, London (1955)

ACTON, H. B. (Editor). (2). *The Philosophy of Punishment,* Macmillan, London (1969)

ANSCOMBE, G. E. M. *Intention,* Blackwell, Oxford (1957)

ARISTOTLE. (1). *Nicomachean Ethics*

ARISTOTLE. (2). *Politics*

ARMSTRONG, K. G. 'The Retributivist Hits Back', *Mind* **70,** 471-490 (1961)

ARON, R. *Main Currents in Sociological Thought* volume 1 (translated by Richard Howard and Helen Weaver), Weidenfeld and Nicolson, London (1965)

AUSTIN, J. L. (1). *Philosophical Papers,* Clarendon Press, Oxford (1961)

AUSTIN, J. L. (2). *Sense and Sensibilia,* Clarendon Press, Oxford (1962)

AYER, A. J. (1). 'Can There be a Private Language?', *Proceedings of the Aristotelian Society,* Supplementary Volume **28,** 63-76 (1954)

AYER, A. J. (2). *Man as a Subject for Science.* Auguste Comte Memorial Lecture 6, Athlone Press, London (1964). Reprinted in Laslett and Runciman (2)

BARRY, B. *Political Argument,* Routledge and Kegan Paul, London (1965)

BELL, D. 'The Idea of a Social Science', *Proceedings of the Aristotelian Society,* Supplementary Volume **41,** 120-132 (1967)

BENN, S. I. 'An Approach to the Problems of Punishment', *Philosophy* **33,** 325-341 (1958)

BENN, S. I. and Peters, R. S. *Social Principles and the Democratic State,* Allen and Unwin, London (1959)

BENTHAM, J. *A Fragment on Government,* and *An Introduction to the Principles of Morals and Legislation* (edited by W. Harrison), Blackwell, Oxford (1948)

BERLIN, I. *Four Essays on Liberty,* Oxford University Press, London (1969)

BRODBECK, M. (Editor). *Readings in the Philosophy of the Social Sciences,* Macmillan Company, New York (1968)

CAMPBELL, C. A. *In Defence of Free Will,* Allen and Unwin, London (1967)

CORNFORTH, M. *The Open Philosophy and the Open Society,* Lawrence and Wishart, London (1968)

COWLING, M. *Mill and Liberalism,* University Press, Cambridge (1963)

CRANSTON, M. *Freedom: A New Analysis,* 3rd edn., Longmans, London (1967)

D'ENTREVES, A. P. *Natural Law,* Hutchinson, London (1951)

DEVLIN, P. *The Enforcement of Morals,* Oxford University Press, London (1968)

EMMET, D. *Rules, Roles and Relations,* Macmillan, London (1966)

ENGELS, F. See Marx

FLEW, A. 'The Justification of Punishment', *Philosophy* **29,** 291-307 (1954)

FOOT, P. (Editor). *Theories of Ethics,* Oxford University Press, London (1967)

FREUD, S. *Two Short Accounts of Psycho-Analysis,* Penguin, Harmondsworth

FRIEDMAN, R. B. 'A New Exploration of Mill's Essay *On Liberty'*, *Political Studies* **14,** 281-304 (1966)

GEACH, P. T. 'Ascriptivism', *Philosophical Review* **69,** 221-225 (1960)

GINSBERG, M. (1). *Essays in Sociology and Social Philosophy,* Penguin, Harmondsworth (1968)

GINSBERG, M. (2). *On Justice in Society,* Penguin, Harmondsworth (1965)

HARE, R. M. (1). *Freedom and Reason,* Clarendon Press, Oxford (1963)

HARE, R. M. (2). *The Language of Morals,* Clarendon Press, Oxford (1952)

HART, H. L. A. (1). 'The Ascription of Responsibility and Rights', *Proceedings of the Aristotelian Society* **49,** 171-194 (1948-49)

HART, H. L. A. (2). *The Concept of Law,* Clarendon Press, Oxford (1961)

HART, H. L. A. (3). *Law, Liberty and Morality,* Oxford University Press, London (1963)

HART, H. L. A. (4). *Punishment and Responsibility,* Clarendon Press, Oxford (1968)

HOBBES, T. *Leviathan*

HUME, D. *A Treatise of Human Nature* (edited by L. A. Selby-Bigge), Clarendon Press, Oxford (1888)

KANT, I. *The Moral Law* (Kant's *Groundwork of the Metaphysic of Morals,* edited by H. J. Paton), Hutchinson, London (n.d.)

KENNY, A. *Action, Emotion and Will,* Routledge and Kegan Paul, London (1963)

LASLETT, P. (1). (Editor). *Philosophy, Politics and Society,* First Series, Blackwell, Oxford (1956)

LASLETT, P. (2). *The World We Have Lost,* Methuen, London (1965)

LASLETT, P. and RUNCIMAN, W. G. (Editors). (1). *Philosophy, Politics and Society,* Second Series, Blackwell, Oxford (1962)

LASLETT, P. and RUNCIMAN, W. G. (Editors). (2). *Philosophy, Politics and Society,* Third Series, Blackwell, Oxford (1967)

LEWIS, H. D. *Morals and Revelation,* Allen and Unwin, London (1951)

LOCKE, J. *Two Treatises of Government* (edited by Peter Laslett), University Press, Cambridge (1960)

LORENZ, K. *On Aggression,* Methuen, London (1966)

LOUCH, A. R. *Explanation and Human Action,* Blackwell, Oxford (1966)

LUCAS, J. R. *The Principles of Politics,* Clarendon Press, Oxford (1966)

MABBOTT, J. D. *The State and the Citizen,* Hutchinson, London (1948)

MACHIAVELLI, N. *The Prince*

MACINTYRE, A. (1). 'The Idea of a Social Science', *Proceedings of the Aristotelian Society,* Supplementary Volume **41,** 95-119 (1967)

MACINTYRE, A. (2). *A Short History of Ethics,* Routledge and Kegan Paul, London (1967)

MACKENZIE, P. T. 'Fact and Value', *Mind* **76,** 228-237 (1967)

MACPHERSON, C. B. *The Political Theory of Possessive Individualism,* Clarendon Press, Oxford (1962)

McPHERSON, T. *Political Obligation,* Routledge and Kegan Paul, London (1967)

MALCOLM, N. *Knowledge and Certainty,* Prentice-Hall, Englewood Cliffs, N.J. (1963)

MARX, K. *Economic and Philosophic Manuscripts of 1844* (translated by M. Milligan), Lawrence and Wishart, London (1959)

MARX, K. and ENGELS, F. *Selected Works,* in two volumes, Foreign Languages Publishing House, Moscow (1962)

MATTHEWS, G. 'Weakness of Will', *Mind* 75, 405-419 (1966)

MELDEN, A. I. *Free Action,* Routledge and Kegan Paul, London (1961)

MILL, J. S. *Utilitarianism, Liberty,* and *Representative Government,* Dent, London (1910)

MITCHELL, B. *Law, Morality, and Religion in a Secular Society,* Oxford University Press, London (1967)

MOBERLY, W. *The Ethics of Punishment,* Faber, London (1968)

MOORE, G. E. (1). *Ethics,* Oxford University Press, London (1945)

MOORE, G. E. (2). *Principia Ethica,* University Press, Cambridge (1903)

MYRDAL, G. *Value in Social Theory,* Routledge and Kegan Paul, London (1958)

NOWELL-SMITH, P. H. *Ethics,* Penguin, Harmondsworth (1954)

OAKESHOTT, M. *Rationalism in Politics,* Methuen, London (1962)

PLAMENATZ, J. (1). *The English Utilitarians,* 2nd edn., Blackwell, Oxford (1958)

PLAMENATZ, J. (2). *Man and Society,* in two volumes, Longmans, London (1963)

PLATO. *Republic*

POPPER, K. R. (1). *Conjectures and Refutations,* 2nd edn., Routledge and Kegan Paul, London (1965)

POPPER, K. R. (2). *The Logic of Scientific Discovery,* Hutchinson, London (1959)

POPPER, K. R. (3). *The Open Society and Its Enemies,* in two volumes, Routledge and Kegan Paul, London (1945)

POPPER, K. R. (4). *The Poverty of Historicism,* Routledge and Kegan Paul, London (1961)

QUINTON, A. (Editor). *Political Philosophy,* Oxford University Press, London (1967)

RAPHAEL, D. D. (Editor). *Political Theory and the Rights of Man,* Macmillan, London (1967)

RASHDALL, H. *The Theory of Good and Evil,* in two volumes, 2nd edn., Oxford University Press, London (1924)

RHEES, R. 'Can There be a Private Language?' *Proceedings of the Aristotelian Society,* Supplementary Volume 28, 77-94 (1954)

ROUSSEAU, J. J. *The Social Contract*

RUNCIMAN, W. G. *Social Science and Political Theory,* University Press, Cambridge (1963)

SIDGWICK, H. *The Methods of Ethics,* 7th edn., Macmillan, London (1907)

STEVENSON, C. L. *Ethics and Language,* Yale University Press, New Haven (1944)

STOCKS, J. L. *Morality and Purpose,* Routledge and Kegan Paul, London (1969)

STRAWSON, P. F. (1). *Introduction to Logical Theory,* Methuen, London (1952)

STRAWSON, P. F. (2). Review of Wittgenstein's *Philosophical Investigations, Mind* 63, 70-99 (1954)

STRAWSON, P. F. (3). 'Social Morality and Individual Ideal', *Philosophy* **36**, 1-17 (1961)

WARNOCK, G. *Contemporary Moral Philosophy,* Macmillan, London (1967)

WARNOCK, M. *Ethics Since 1900,* Oxford University Press, London (1960)

WEBER, M. *The Theory of Social and Economic Organization,* (trans. A. M. Henderson and Talcott Parsons), The Free Press, Glencoe, Illinois (1947)

WHITE, A. R. (Editor). *The Philosophy of Action,* Oxford University Press, London (1968)

WILLIAMSON, C. 'Ideology and the Problem of Knowledge', *Inquiry* **10**, 121-138 (1967)

WINCH, P. (1). *The Idea of a Social Science,* Routledge and Kegan Paul, London (1958)

WINCH, P. (2). 'Mr. Louch's Idea of a Social Science', *Inquiry* **7**, 202-208 (1964)

WINCH, P. (3). 'Understanding a Primitive Society', *American Philosophical Quarterly* **1**, 307-324 (1964)

WITTGENSTEIN, L. *Philosophical Investigations* (trans. G. E. M. Anscombe, 2nd edn.,), Blackwell, Oxford (1958)

WOOTTON, B. *Social Science and Social Pathology,* Allen and Unwin, London (1959)

# Index